Edith Patterson Meyer,

first a librarian, then an editor, now finds time to travel and write. In the last few years she has visited Ireland, Italy, Greece and Scandinavia, and has traveled across the United States and to Hawaii.

Her earlier books have been about people: the story of Alfred Nobel, DYNAMITE AND PEACE; profiles of the winners of the Nobel Peace Prize, CHAMPIONS OF PEACE; and the life of Grania O'Malley, PIRATE QUEEN. In THE FRIENDLY FRONTIER she has made equally real the story of the Canadian-United States border, and in MEET THE FUTURE she shows the major role played by libraries and librarians in the modern world.

Her CHAMPIONS OF THE FOUR FREEDOMS is a biographical approach to the beginnings and continuation of the American struggle toward these essential rights of man.

CHAMPIONS of the FOUR FREEDOMS

by EDITH PATTERSON MEYER

Here are short biographies of men and institutions that have been in the forefront of the fight to establish and maintain the freedoms which President Franklin D. Roosevelt enumerated during World War II. The struggle to secure the rights of freedom of speech and religion and freedom from want and fear had begun centuries before that, and men had fought and died for them in this country even before the Revolutionary War.

So this book begins with John Peter Zenger, who went to jail for printing a newspaper critical of the New York governor of the 1730's. It ends with the efforts of the Peace Corps toward freedom from want, and of the United Nations toward freedom from fear. Its significant personalities of this century include Julia Lathrop of the Children's Bureau, the plant wizard, George Washington Carver, the scientist Linus Pauling, the civil rights leader, Martin Luther King, and Mr. and Mrs. F.D.R.

Many of the earlier Americans herein are less known to American students. It is to be hoped that inspiration as well as information will be gained by becoming acquainted with all of them.

BOOKS by EDITH PATTERSON MEYER

DYNAMITE and PEACE
The Story of Alfred Nobel

CHAMPIONS of PEACE
Winners of the Nobel Peace Prize

PIRATE QUEEN
The Story of Ireland's Grania O'Malley
in the Days of Queen Elizabeth

THE FRIENDLY FRONTIER
The Story of the Canadian-American Border

MEET the FUTURE
People and Ideas in the Libraries
of Today and Tomorrow

CHAMPIONS of the FOUR FREEDOMS

CHAMPIONS OF

THE FOUR FREEDOMS

The Death of Elijah P. Lovejoy from a contemporary woodcut

CHAMPIONS of the FOUR FREEDOMS

by Edith Patterson Meyer

Illustrated by Eric von Schmidt

Little, Brown and Company · Boston · Toronto

LIBRARY OF CONGRESS CATALOG CARD NO. 66–17689

FIRST EDITION

*Published simultaneously in Canada
by Little, Brown & Company (Canada) Limited*

PRINTED IN THE UNITED STATES OF AMERICA

To my friends

— especially Alice —

who encouraged me

in the writing of this book

Where the mind is without fear and
the head is held high;
  Where knowledge is free;
  Where the world has not been broken
up into fragments by narrow domestic walls;
  Where words come out from the depth of truth;
  Where tireless striving stretches its arms
towards perfection;
  Where the clear stream of reason has not
lost its way into the dreary desert sand of
dead habit;
  Where the mind is led forward by Thee
into ever-widening thought and action—
  Into that heaven of freedom, my Father,
let my country awake.

RABINDRANATH TAGORE

Foreword

WE in the United States of America talk and write a good deal about freedom. We say we live in the "land of the free" and we sing, "Let freedom ring!" But we very seldom stop to think what these things mean, or how they came about, or who had a hand in making America the "land of the free."

According to Zechariah Chafee, an American professor of law, our freedoms "were not found under a gooseberry bush. They were shaped and achieved through centuries of struggle, through the willingness of men to languish in prison and die there, through long thinking and endless tedious work."

America has a proud list of champions of freedom. It extends all the way from the early colonial days to the present time. High on that list are our founding fathers, whose "long thinking and endless tedious work" mapped out a guide to help protect our freedoms — our Constitution, with its Bill of Rights.

Yet, as the poet Archibald MacLeish tells us, even in a democratic nation like ours, "Freedom is never an accomplished fact. It is always a process." Chief Justice Earl Warren warns, "Every generation must preserve its own freedoms." And President Franklin D. Roosevelt said much the same thing in 1936 at the anniversary of the dedication of the Statue of Liberty: "Liberty and peace are living things. In each generation — if they are to be maintained — they must be guarded and vitalized anew."

When President Roosevelt made his State of the Nation address to Congress five years later the world was darkened by war. But the President looked beyond the war years to a time of peace and a world of brotherhood. That world, he said, would be founded on four essential freedoms:

The first is freedom of speech and expression — everywhere in the world.

The second is freedom of every person to worship God in his own way — everywhere in the world.

The third is freedom from want, which, translated into world terms, means economic understandings which will secure to every nation a healthy peacetime life for its inhabitants — everywhere in the world.

The fourth is freedom from fear, which, translated into world terms, means a worldwide reduction of armaments to such a point and in such a thorough fashion that no nation will be in a position to commit an act of physical aggression against any neighbor — anywhere in the world.

The following pages tell a little about a few of the champions of these Four Freedoms.

Contents

Appendices

I

THE FIRST IS
FREEDOM OF SPEECH
AND EXPRESSION

The great American word is freedom, and in particular freedom of thought, speech, and assembly. ROBERT M. HUTCHINS

IN A SENSE, *all freedoms are a single freedom, one and indivisible. The First Amendment to our Constitution lumps together in one short breath freedom of religion, of speech and the press, of assembly, and of petition. Yet it is possible to pick apart the fabric of freedom and examine its strands, one by one.*

To many persons freedom of speech seems the most important strand. It includes not just the words that come out of a person's mouth but the freedom to think the thoughts behind the words, and the freedom to put them down on paper or to express them in some other way. In America "speaking one's mind" is considered everyone's privilege. But some people who believe strongly in free speech for themselves are not at all tolerant of free speech for others, especially if the ideas expressed differ from their own. They don't enjoy listening to what they don't agree with. Yet, as the English writer John Stuart Mill pointed out a century ago, "Sometimes we come, on further reflection, to find merit in the new idea; and if we do not, we understand our own views better by testing them against different views."

Americans have learned that human progress depends on the free expression of different ideas and opinions. "Tolerating dissent" is the American way. But even today people who are afraid of progress, afraid of change, are likely to oppose this. And so freedom of speech still needs its champions — champions as daring and forthright as Peter Zenger, George Mason, Elijah Lovejoy, Oliver Wendell Holmes, Jr., and those others who bravely followed their example.

Liberty of the press is . . . a restraint to evil government.

Unwilted Under Persecution

John Peter Zenger (1697–1746)

THIRTEEN-YEAR-OLD John Peter Zenger stood beside the rail watching the sailors tie the wooden sailing vessel to the little New York dock. This New World city did not look much like London, or even Rotterdam! Peter hoped it would bring better days than either of those cities had brought to the Zengers and the two hundred other German immigrants England's Queen Anne had sent to America.

Peter's father had died of fever on the long voyage, and

Peter felt responsible for his mother and younger brother and sister. Was he strong enough to take his father's place? Would the authorities let him go with the men into the forests to tap trees for turpentine and cut down tall pines for masts?

Peter joined his mother, ten-year-old John, and the little sister as colonial officers came aboard to inspect and direct the immigrants. Soon the newcomers were put ashore and led to a sort of tent town set up in an open field. It was a crude way to live, though better than on the crowded ship. Better — until typhoid broke out. Then the immigrants were hastily transferred to an island in the harbor, and the sturdy men with families were sent up the Hudson, where they would clear land, build houses, and work in the pine woods.

Peter was not allowed to go with them, but the necessary fees would be paid to apprentice him and young John to a trade. William Bradford needed an apprentice in his printing shop, the Governor's representative told Peter. Would he like that?

Peter's face brightened. In his wanderings about the town he had noticed the sign, shaped like an open book, swinging above William Bradford's printing-shop door and had stopped to peer through the small-paned windows at the two wooden presses on the floor inside. He had stared curiously at the damp paper sheets strung like a wash to dry on wires stretched head-high across the room and sniffed the smell of fresh ink. He would like nothing better than to work in that printing shop!

Mrs. Zenger gladly signed the official paper binding Peter to William Bradford for eight years to learn the printer's trade. Then she signed another paper which bound John as an apprentice to a carpenter. She and her daughter were to live in a Dutch household, where she would help the hausfrau with her work.

Peter soon became almost like one of the Bradford family. William Bradford helped his new apprentice master the printing skills and improve his English. At night the apprentices all went to school, as the law required, to study reading, writing, and arithmetic. Peter was a good worker and quick to learn. Before long English came as easily to his tongue as his native German, and he could set type, operate the great wooden presses, and fold the printed sheets.

It was a busy shop, for William Bradford was one of the best printers in the colonies. He did the official printing for the New York colony and published almanacs, prayer books, a few general books, and miscellaneous pamphlets; he also sold books that he imported from England, France, and the Netherlands. Mrs. Bradford, a pleasant Quaker lady, ran the household and kept the books for the firm. She became fond of Peter, and he, after a time, lost his solemn ways and began to smile, to sing at his work, and even to joke.

The eight years of apprenticeship went by quickly. At twenty-one, Peter was ready to go out on his own. He decided to travel to Maryland and try to become the official printer for that colony, as Mr. Bradford was for New York. But after a short time in the Southern colony his young wife died, leaving a baby boy, and Peter returned to his family and friends in New York. For a while he worked again in William Bradford's shop, even becoming a partner. Then, seeing that there was plenty of work for a second printing shop in New York, Peter decided to become established in his own right. He had married again, a capable girl of Dutch descent. And he had become a freeman — a voting citizen — of the city.

From the start, Peter's little shop was busy. His wife Anna helped him in it. They did small printing jobs for individuals and many religious tracts, most of them in Dutch, for church societies. In 1730, Peter Zenger published the first arithmetic book printed in the colony.

New York had a new governor — a greedy, high-handed man not above using unscrupulous means to win his way. Since 1725, William Bradford had published a weekly newspaper, the *New York Gazette*. Naturally, being the official royal printer, he was expected to represent the Governor's point of view. The *Gazette* could not criticize Governor Cosby's rather shady transactions, which involved bribes, confiscation of land, and rigged elections. These things, however, worried many of the leading citizens. Several of them, including some lawyers, came to Peter Zenger to ask him to start a weekly paper which would take the side of the opposition. They promised to finance the paper and to contribute articles under fictitious names.

Zenger agreed. In November 1733 he printed the first issue of the *New York Weekly Journal*. People bought it eagerly to read its news items, its letters from Europe, its jokes, poems, and articles. Some of these pointed out the responsibilities of all good citizens, as well as of persons in power, to improve the government. The *Journal* quite openly criticized several officials. It even dared hint that it would be a good thing for the colony if Governor Cosby were recalled to England to account for his misgovernment.

The Governor read the *Journal's* pages with increasing concern. When he saw such statements as "Liberty of the press is a curb, a bridle, a terror, a snare, and a restraint to evil government," he decided to put an end to the *Journal* before it put an end to him! The writers of the critical articles and jeering verses could not be reached because their contributions were either unsigned or signed with pen names, but the editor-publisher was legally responsible for what he printed. Punishing Peter Zenger, the Governor calculated, would undoubtedly finish the *Journal*.

After a whole year of publishing the *Journal* without trouble things suddenly began to happen. First a reward was offered to anyone who would reveal the identity of the authors of some of the *Journal* items the Governor objected to. When this brought no result, the Governor ordered four issues of the paper, which contained certain "scandalous reflections" and "scandalous ballads," to be publicly burned by the colony's hangman or whipper. But this official came under the control of the New York Assembly, and the Assembly forbade him to carry out the Governor's order. The burning was finally done, but it was not the great spectacle the Governor had planned. The sheriff's slave lit the fire and only the Governor and a few hangers-on were present.

The next Sunday Governor Cosby had Peter Zenger arrested and put into the city jail. On Monday, to the Governor's delight, the *Journal* did not make its usual appearance. It was the first time it missed publication — and the last. The following Monday the *Journal* appeared as usual. It contained an explanation by Peter Zenger. The paper had not come out the previous week, he wrote, because he had been arrested and imprisoned and for several days had not been allowed to see anyone or to have pen, ink, or paper. Now that he was permitted "the Liberty of Speaking through the Hole of the Door" to his wife and servants, he promised to try "to entertain you with my weekly *Journal* as formerly."

Governor Cosby's officers fixed Zenger's bail so high that it was impossible for him to pay it, and he had to stay on in jail. Yet, to the Governor's dismay and the New Yorkers' delight, the paper was published each week. Thanks to Peter's persistence, to Anna's faithfulness, industry, and skill, and to the contributions of the unnamed writers, the *Journal* went on entertaining and informing the people, commenting on the Governor's misdeeds, and pointing out glaring examples of bad administration.

When the court hearing finally came up, the jury could find nothing against Zenger. But instead of releasing him, the attorney general, on the Governor's order, filed an "information charge" against him for printing "false, scandalous, and seditious libels." For this he must stand trial in the following session of the court, three months later. So poor Peter stayed in jail all winter, uncomfortable and unhappy, but "unwilted under persecution." Each day he passed material and instructions to his wife through the "Hole of the Door," and each week the *Journal* made its appearance.

Two very good lawyers were to defend Zenger at the April trial. One of them, James Alexander, was almost certainly the author of many of the *Journal's* critical articles. But when these two lawyers dared to protest the choice of judges appointed to hear the trial, they were abruptly disbarred and the trial held over until the court met again in August. Once more Peter had no choice but to remain in jail. And in place of two experienced lawyers he now had only a new, inexperienced counsel appointed to his case by the court.

The disbarred lawyers were not idle. They made a trip to Philadelphia, where they called on an elderly Quaker gentleman by the name of Andrew Hamilton. Mr. Hamilton was one of America's most distinguished lawyers, known for his staunch support of the people's rights. He was a member of the Pennsylvania Assembly, architect of the State House one day to be known as Independence Hall, friend of Benjamin Franklin, and one-time attorney for William Penn. Like James Alexander, he was a Scotsman, trained in law in England. On their return to New York the two lawyers told only Peter that they had turned over to Mr. Hamilton their arguments for the case, and that he had agreed to come to New York to represent him in court.

On the warm August day of the trial the courtroom was crowded with members of the Governor's party and with townspeople friendly to Zenger. The court tried to choose the jury from a selected list of persons who favored the Governor, but Peter's young lawyer quickly stopped this, insisting that the court select the jury from the complete list of voters.

As the session began, there was a stir in the courtroom. People turned to see Mr. Alexander enter and escort to the front a rather feeble-looking, formally dressed, bewigged old gentleman, whom he presented to the court as special

counsel for the defense. In answer to the clerk's usual
questions, the visitor gave his name as Andrew Hamilton,
Esquire, and stated that he had been admitted to the bar in
England. An air of excitement filled the room as Mr.
Hamilton shook hands with Mr. Zenger and sat down
beside him.

The attorney general read several items which he
charged Peter Zenger had printed and published in the *New
York Weekly Journal*. He called them "false, scandalous,
and seditious libels against the Government." The court, he
said, was ready to prove the prisoner's guilt.

To everyone's surprise, Mr. Hamilton agreed without
argument that Mr. Zenger had printed and published the
items read. "I hope that in doing so he has committed no
crime," Mr. Hamilton said, adding that publishing a complaint was the right of any citizen "when the matter so
published can be supported with truth."

The attorney general objected. According to law, he
said, a complaint was no less a libel if true. And since the
defense had admitted the publication of the items in question, there would be no need of the witnesses who were
present merely to prove that point, so he hereby dismissed
them. Turning to the jurors, he said they had only to find
the prisoner guilty of publishing the items under question;
the court would decide whether or not they were libelous.

No, said Andrew Hamilton firmly; it was not that simple.
The mere publishing of statements in a newspaper was not a
crime. A man had a right to complain against injustice and
the abuse of power. The Government was not libeled by
having the truth told about it. Mr. Zenger's statements must
be proved to be "false, scandalous, and seditious, or else we
are not guilty." Moreover, it was the jury's right to inquire

into evidence of truth or falsehood, and the defense would present witnesses to establish the truth of the statements in the *Journal.*

The chief justice and attorney general were on a spot. They did not dare permit the defense to call witnesses, for who knew what might be testified about the Governor! And the jurors, like most New Yorkers, would know whether or not what was said was true! So the court began a long discussion with Mr. Hamilton on the legal definition of libel. Any complaint against the Government, they claimed, was libel, and they referred to cases in English law to prove their point.

The decisions in the cases they cited, Mr. Hamilton objected, were outlawed, replaced by a newer idea which was rapidly becoming accepted both in England and in its colonies. That newer idea was that people had a right to air their grievances; that open political discussion and freedom of the press were an essential part of a progressive society.

Everyone in the courtroom was impressed by Mr. Hamilton's argument and by the quiet yet eloquent way he presented it. No wonder that the expression "as smart as a Philadelphia lawyer" originated with Andrew Hamilton's defense of Peter Zenger! He based the whole case on two great principles — that truth could be used as a defense, and that the jury had a right to decide not only on the facts of the matter but also on the law.

The court continued to refuse to allow the defense to present witnesses, even objecting to any further argument on the point. At that, Mr. Hamilton turned to the jury. In a magnificent speech he appealed to the jurors to take matters into their own hands. "Free men have a right to complain when hurt," he told them. "They have a right to oppose arbitrary power by speaking and writing truths . . . to assert with courage the sense they have of the blessings of liberty, the value they put upon it, and their resolution at all hazards to prove it one of the greatest blessings heaven can bestow."

And he declared, "The question before the court and you, Gentlemen of the Jury, is not of small or private concern. It is not the cause of one poor printer, nor of New York alone, which you are now trying. No! It may in its consequences affect every freeman that lives under a British government, on the main of America. It is the best cause; it is the cause of liberty."

The attorney general tried to weaken the effect of Mr. Hamilton's words by remarking that the counsel for the defense had gone out of the way in his eloquence. All the jury had to do, he repeated, was to find the defendant guilty; the jurors should leave matters of law to the court.

The jury filed out of the room. They were gone only a short time. The crowd in the courtroom stirred excitedly when they returned and the clerk asked, "Has the jury reached a verdict?"

"We have," the foreman of the jury answered. "Not guilty."

"Upon which," wrote Peter Zenger in his account of the trial the next week in the *Journal,* "there were three huzzas in the hall, which was crowded with people; and the next day I was discharged from my imprisonment."

There were considerably more than "three huzzas." The court could not restrain the people. They laughed and they shouted. For the moment Peter Zenger was forgotten, and

Andrew Hamilton was their hero. They carried him on their shoulders to his inn, where they wined and dined him and gave him the keys to the city in appreciation of the services he had rendered its citizens "by his learned and generous defence of the rights of mankind and the liberty of the press in the case of John Peter Zenger." And the next morning they fired a salute of guns to the distinguished lawyer as he boarded a barge to cross the North River on his journey back to Philadelphia.

Peter Zenger's acquittal was a crushing defeat for Governor Cosby and his political friends. It was much more. Because of it, said Livingston Rutherfurd in writing of the Zenger trial, "the people became equipped with the most powerful weapon for successfully combatting arbitrary power, the right of freely criticizing the conduct of public men." And because of Andrew Hamilton's defense of Peter Zenger, liberty of the press became a fact in America more than fifty years earlier than in England.

As an expression of confidence, Zenger was made public printer for the New York colony in 1737. The next year he became public printer also for New Jersey. For several years, until his too-early death, he continued to publish the *New York Weekly Journal*. His widow Anna carried it on for two years, and John Zenger, Peter's son by his first wife, for three years after that.

Peter Zenger's claim to fame rests on his unswerving pursuit of a free press, even at the cost of personal discomfort and suffering. "The trial of Zenger in 1735," said the American statesman Gouverneur Morris, "was the germ of American freedom, the morning star of that liberty which subsequently revolutionized America."

Freedom of the press is one of the great bulwarks of liberty.

Reluctant Statesman

George Mason (1725–1792)

AT THE TIME of Peter Zenger's trial in 1735, ten-year-old George Mason had just lost his father, drowned when his sailboat capsized in the choppy Potomac River near his home in Virginia. The boy's guardians were his mother and an uncle who lived a little farther down the river. This uncle was a lawyer and a scholar, with one of the best libraries in all the colonies. Thanks as much to it as to his tutors, George Mason acquired an excellent education. He had a quick, logical mind and a natural fondness for books. Poring over the legal volumes in his uncle's library gave him such familiarity with the history, principles, and procedures of law that, though he never became a lawyer, he was consulted all his life as an authority on matters of law.

The Virginia colony had come a long way in the hundred years since its royal Governor, William Berkeley, bragged that there were no free schools and no free press in his colony and he hoped there never would be. The Virginia that George Mason grew up in had become one of the most progressive of the American colonies. George's friends were the sons and daughters of highly cultivated English-American planters who lived in elegant style on their broad tobacco-growing plantations in the tidewater section of Virginia. Ships, often the planters' own, took the tobacco across the Atlantic to England and on returning brought books, clothing, furniture, and luxuries from London. Many of the young people went to England to school. Others, like George Mason, were educated at home by English tutors. These young Virginians hunted and raced, fenced, entertained and were entertained, but they also had serious discussions about their colony and its future. They talked about the settling of the rich western "back country," about the French and Indian Wars; about the Assembly at Williamsburg and how it was being changed by the growing number of small farmers in the colony.

In his early twenties George Mason took over the management of the family plantation. He enjoyed the responsibility, and he soon showed that he was an excellent agriculturist and a sound businessman. With his large, powerful body, his dark hair and black eyes set in a good-looking, rather serious face, he made a dashing figure as he rode horseback, hunted, or danced. He liked to buy pieces of land to add to the family property, and more than once he and his friend and neighbor George Washington rode out together to survey the boundaries of some adjoining properties. But with all his strenuous outdoor life and many social activities, George Mason still found time for serious reading and thinking.

When he was twenty-five, George married an attractive girl from the Maryland colony across the Potomac. They built a fine house on Dogue's Neck, naming it Gunston Hall in honor of the English place George's mother's people had come from. The young couple exchanged visits with the neighboring Lees and Carters and Washingtons. George was active in the parish church and in the affairs of Fairfax County and the newly established town of Alexandria. He was financially interested, too, in the Ohio Company, formed to develop western lands, to trade with the Indians, and to move settlers over the mountains. He went to the meetings of the Alexandria trustees, and to the monthly sessions of the Fairfax County Court, but he would not consider becoming a member of the Virginia Assembly. He saw no good reason for making the long and tiresome journey to Williamsburg and being away for weeks at a time from his wife and growing family, his comfortable home, and his prosperous plantation. He had, he admitted, "no stomach for any sort of political intrigue," and he quickly became irritated by "the stupidity of human nature in committee." Besides, he was beginning to be troubled by frequent painful attacks of gouty arthritis, which were not much relieved by bloodletting or the other remedies of the time. The quiet atmosphere of his study, the routine work of managing the plantation, and his local activities suited him very well.

It was the 1765 Stamp Act that turned George Mason into a "reluctant statesman." Like George Washington, Richard Henry Lee, and Patrick Henry, he felt that the colonists' rights as freeborn British subjects were being trampled on when they had to obey laws which they had not consented to through freely chosen representatives. In an open letter to the *London Public Ledger,* addressed to British businessmen, Mason expressed his deep concern over this matter and the strained British-American relations it was causing. He predicted that Americans, brought up in the English-law principles of freedom, would not submit to such oppression for very long. "We owe our Mother Country the duty of subjects," he wrote; "we will not pay her the submission of slaves."

Like other Virginians, Mason wanted nothing more than to clear up the trouble with England quickly. He found a legally sound way around using the hated tax stamps and worked out a plan to boycott British-taxed goods. He called these measures "Non-Importation Resolves" and asked Washington to take them to the Virginia Assembly for discussion.

When the burgesses — the members of the Assembly — dared to object to the British taxation, the royal Governor of Virginia dissolved the Assembly. The burgesses refused to be silenced. They moved over to Raleigh Tavern and continued the session "on their own." When George Washington read to them Mason's Resolves, the burgesses voted in favor of them.

As America slowly but surely moved toward war with Britain, Mason became less the plantation gentleman and more the active statesman. When the British closed the port of Boston, he and Washington started a subscription fund to aid Bostonians. He helped organize the Fairfax County militia, supposedly in case of trouble with the Indians, and along with Washington he was outfitted in its uniform, later to become that of the Continental Army — blue coat piped in buff, buff waistcoat and breeches, and white stockings. Mason addressed the citizens of Fairfax County on the trouble with England, stating his belief that every Government's power "was originally lodged in and consequently is derived from the people," and that government existed "for the general good and safety of the community."

During the worry-filled summer of 1774, when war was becoming a fact, George Mason sat in his study at Gunston Hall and wrote a masterly statement of the colonies' grounds for opposition to the Crown. He recommended calling a congress of representatives from all the colonies "to concert a general and uniform plan for the defense and preservation of our common rights." He also recommended stopping all exports to Great Britain, particularly tobacco and lumber, unless the taxation wrongs were speedily corrected. This statement, known as the Fairfax Resolves, was adopted first by Fairfax County, then by the Virginia Assembly, and later by the Continental Congress, when it met as Mason had recommended.

When this Congress appointed George Washington commander-in-chief of the Continental Army, George Mason agreed to take his friend's place in the Virginia Assembly. Dissolved for a second time, it now called itself the Virginia Convention and was meeting in Richmond.

Mason did not enjoy attending the Convention. His

quick mind found it "ill conducted" and tedious. The daily meetings of the Committee of Safety, to which he was appointed, irritated him so much that they literally made him ill. Yet he attended them regularly and did much to help plan the colony's military preparation.

America was now moving toward independence. Tom Paine's dream of freedom as expressed in his fiery *Common Sense* swept the country. In May 1775, the Virginia Convention instructed its delegates to the Continental Congress at Philadelphia to propose that the Congress prepare a statement of rights and declare the United Colonies free and independent states.

Throwing off British rule made it necessary for the individual colonies — or states, as they would now become — to set up their own Governments. The Virginia Convention appointed a committee to work out a constitution for the new state of Virginia. Patrick Henry and James Madison were on the committee, and George Mason was made its head as soon as he arrived — late, because of "a smart fit of the gout."

This was the moment for which George Mason had been preparing from the boyhood day when he first stepped into his uncle's library! He was steeped in the history and traditions of English law, yet deeply convinced that men were born with certain basic rights, and that Governments existed to serve the people. The idea of building an independent democratic society in the New World fired him with enthusiasm. "We are now going upon the most important of all subjects — government!" he wrote a friend. The revolt against Great Britain, he said, was "nothing compared to the Great Business now before us."

The first thing needed, George Mason said as he pitched headlong into that "Great Business," was "a statement of those rights held by all people, individually and in association with others." To prepare this statement, he made notes and more notes, consulted law books, covered pages of foolscap with drafts and yet more drafts. The weather was muggy; his gout bothered him; he felt impatient and inadequate — and burning with a kind of inspiration. He worked feverishly to bring to life a dream of "a new kind of society — fresh, equal, just, open, free."

In less than a week George Mason presented to his committee his Declaration of Rights. It was "clear, comprehensive, and faultlessly expressed." The committee made only a few minor changes in the ten basic articles, then had the document printed and distributed for the delegates to study. Point by point it was debated on the Convention floor, and in two weeks time, on June 12, 1776, the Convention unanimously adopted the Virginia Declaration, or Bill, of Rights. Seventeen days later it approved the state Constitution, most of which was also Mason's work.

With the adoption of the Declaration and the Constitution, Virginians were no longer subjects of Great Britain but citizens of a new state. They were assured of their birthright as free Americans and of "man's native freedom from restraint unless he threatened or did harm to others." The relationship between the people and their Government was clearly based on the belief that free men were capable of maintaining an orderly Government which would work for, and be responsible to, the people.

The most basic of the freedoms covered in the Virginia Declaration of Rights was that of freedom of speech and the press. Never before had a Government guaranteed this to its people. Under it, printers and publishers need no longer worry for fear the local sheriff might not have heard of the Zenger case, and individual citizens need not dread being punished for criticizing an official. In the Virginia Declaration of Rights they read that ". . . freedom of the press is one of the great bulwarks of liberty and can never be restrained but by despotic governments."

Free speech and a free press, said George Mason, would safeguard and promote the cause of freedom by helping correct faults in the democracy and by opening the way to improvement and progress. Other colonies — Massachusetts in particular — had been struggling toward this idea, but George Mason was the first to express it, and Virginia was the first state to make it into law.

In Philadelphia, Thomas Jefferson, one of Virginia's delegates to the Continental Congress, borrowed from the Virginia Declaration of Rights in drafting his preamble to the Declaration of Independence. All up and down the Eastern seaboard colonial newspapers printed the Virginia Declaration, and many of the colonies followed it in writing their constitutions, sometimes almost word for word. Across the Atlantic, France used it in its world-shaking Declaration of the Rights of Man.

George Mason, retiring and personally unambitious, did not claim for himself the credit he deserved, but Thomas Jefferson paid him tribute in these words: "The fact is unquestionable that the Bill of Rights and the Constitution of Virginia were drawn originally by George Mason, one of our really great men and of the first order of greatness." He was, said one of his associates, a man who "from his entrance into public life was confessedly the first man in every assembly of which he was a member."

Mason's attendance at the new Assembly was irregular because of his health and because his wife had died, leaving him with a large family to look after. No doubt also because of his distaste for legislative duties! The other Fairfax County delegate complained that Mason's presence was needed, for his influence was great and his fellow delegates listened respectfully when he spoke. This was not surprising, for, as Jefferson commented, "his eloquence was neither flowing nor smooth, but his language was sharp, his manner most impressive, and strengthened by a dash of biting cynicism when provocation made it seasonable."

Mason truly believed he could do more for his state and country at home than in the Assembly. He worked early and late in his Gunston Hall study, carrying on a heavy correspondence with leaders in Virginia and at the Continental Congress. His door was never closed to those who rode up the cherry-shaded lane to consult him, and there were many. When the Assembly made Patrick Henry Virginia's first Governor, George Mason helped him put the new state Constitution into action, making new laws and reorganizing courts. Mason even had a hand in designing the great seal of the Commonwealth of Virginia.

Although Virginia always came first in George Mason's affections, he was deeply concerned about the problems that faced the struggling new nation. The Continental Congress had few powers; the paper money it issued was so nearly worthless that Mason said, "I would almost as soon receive payment for a sum of money in a bundle of last Year's News-Papers." The war was going badly. A discouraged Washington wrote Mason that the country's military organization was nearly as weak as its financial position. The states were more powerful than the central Government. Jealous of one another's power, they pulled in one direction and another. Most of them had not signed the Articles of Confederation set up soon after the signing of the Declaration of Independence.

To help strengthen the finances of the federal Government, Mason suggested that Virginia cede to it the state's vast holdings in the "back country." He helped arrange the transfer, even though it meant personal sacrifice to him, for he had invested heavily in western lands. Other states followed Virginia's example, giving up their western holdings to the nation.

The final year of the war was one of especial stress and strain for George Mason and his neighbors, for the British were active all along the Virginia coastline. In Mason's own Fairfax County they burned warehouses, plundered estates, and kept everyone in a constant state of alarm. Twice British troops came up the Potomac bent on burning Gunston Hall. The first time they were stopped by a bad storm; the second time the Virginia Volunteers turned them back. Mason sent his family across the Potomac, but he stayed at home to work for the state and nation and to help with the defense of Fairfax County. With the coming of the French allies, the war situation became brighter. After the defeat of Cornwallis at Yorktown there were only a few minor campaigns, and in 1783 came the signing of the Treaty of Peace.

The young nation stumbled along, urgently needing a solid Constitution and a firm Government. Mason felt so strongly about this need that, much as he hated to leave his new wife, his growing children, and the peace of Gunston Hall, he agreed to be a delegate to the 1787 Constitutional Convention. He was pleasantly surprised to find the delegates from the other states men of high caliber, stimulating to work with. He entered into the business of the Convention with enthusiasm, attending all sessions and speaking on every important topic. James Madison commented that he impressed the delegates as "a powerful reasoner and a profound statesman."

Like all his neighbors, Mason had slaves on his plantation. Yet he felt that slavery was an inhuman institution and that the Constitution should outlaw "this infernal traffic." He was concerned by the conflict of interests between the increasingly industrial North and the agricultural South, and with the way each played off its advantages against the other. Virginia, he felt, was giving up too much for too little, and the states too much for the federal Government. Most of all, he was concerned about the nation's Constitution not having a Bill of Rights. It was not, he said, complete without it. He could promise that one could be made ready in a few hours, using the various state Declarations. In spite of most states having their own, it would give "great quiet" to the people, for the United States Constitution would be the supreme law of the land, above the state Constitutions.

Mason was voted down on both his proposal for a Bill of Rights and for the gradual abolition of slavery. He felt rebuffed and angry. He had pinned his hopes on this Convention. Now his dreams of guaranteeing freedom of speech and other essential rights to all the citizens of this new country were gone. Discouraged beyond reason, he refused to sign the Constitution and left the Convention in a huff, predicting that the new Government would turn into a monarchy or into a "corrupt, oppressive aristocracy."

To add to his misery, on his way back to Virginia Mason's coach overturned, hurting him rather badly. Still he would not give up. He tried to impress his point of view on his fellow Virginians by speaking, letter-writing, and by publishing a broadside, *Objections to the Constitution*. He went right to the point, beginning, "There is no declaration of rights." He sent the *Objections* to Washington and to other leaders, both in and beyond the state. Patrick Henry agreed with his views, but Washington did not, and a coolness sprang up between the two lifelong friends. Jefferson was in France, where he had been sent to help Benjamin Franklin and John Adams negotiate treaties with European countries and then remained to succeed Franklin as minister to France. When Madison wrote him that Mason "considers the want of a Bill of Rights a fatal objection" to the Constitution, Jefferson answered that he, too, felt that the federal Constitution should include a Bill of Rights. Jefferson had always appreciated Mason and relied on his judgment.

Once again Mason took comfort in his beloved Gunston Hall. He was hurt by the slights of old friends, wearied by unaccustomed exertion, and plagued by attacks of the gout. In his study he wrote many letters, trying desperately to influence leaders to call a second federal convention to make such changes in the Constitution as the various states might recommend. No state, he felt — certainly not Virginia — should ratify the Constitution as it stood.

He still gave plenty of evidence of the sharp wit and the courage for which he was noted. When one critic suggested that his mind must be failing, Mason retorted, "Sir, when yours fails, no one will ever notice it." When someone told him that the people of Alexandria would mob him if he dared to oppose publicly Virginia's ratifying the Constitution, he mounted his horse and rode into town. At the courthouse, says Kate Mason Rowland, he asked the sheriff to "make proclamation that George Mason will address the people." A crowd gathered, and from the courthouse steps Mason "denounced the Constitution with bitter invective, after which he mounted his horse and returned home."

In this heated controversy, James Madison played the role of peacemaker. If, as George Mason claimed, a federal Bill of Rights would quiet the fears of those who opposed the Constitution, why not add such a Bill in the form of Amendments? Using Mason's Virginia Declaration of Rights as a model and adding a little to it, Madison worked out a possible document, then went to Gunston Hall to talk it over with Mason. To his delight, Mason agreed with it in general, although he wanted the Amendments added first, before Virginia ratified the Constitution. And he still hoped that New York and Virginia by working together could force the calling of another convention.

George Mason went to the Virginia Convention to lead the fight against the state's ratification of the federal Constitution. Patrick Henry stood beside him. On June 3, 1788, Mr. Mason addressed the Assembly with — so Kate Mason Rowland tells us — "his once raven hair white as snow, his stalwart figure attired in deep mourning still erect, his black eyes fairly flashing forth the flame that burned in his bosom, the tones of his voice deliberate and full." Everyone listened spellbound to his arguments against ratification.

For a time the result seemed in doubt. Then James Madison arose and argued for ratifying the Constitution with the proviso that a Bill of Rights be appended. He implored the legislators to vote for it, saying it would do no harm if some of them voted "from a spirit of conciliation rather than conviction." Finally, by a narrow margin, Virginia voted to ratify the federal Constitution, with the recommendation that a Bill of Rights be added to it.

George Mason was asked to work out a proposed federal Bill of Rights. He submitted a long, detailed list of Articles, which was whittled down to what was basically his 1776 Virginia Declaration of Rights. Other state conventions suggested other inclusions — more than a hundred amendments in all — but George Mason's draft was the one most closely followed in what became the federal Bill of Rights. Appended to the Constitution in the form of ten Amendments, it was adopted by the first Congress of the United States of America. Ironically Virginia, the first state to have its own Declaration of Rights, was the last to ratify the United States Bill of Rights.

Thomas Jefferson, summoned back from France by the first President to become his Secretary of State, called at Gunston Hall in 1792. He and Mason discussed the affairs of the nation and agreed that much progress had been made. "A man could go to sleep contented with the health of his new government, if not supremely happy about it," George Mason said. And soon afterward he did indeed go to sleep, forever.

I know that I have the right to speak and publish my sentiments, subject only to the laws of the land for the abuse of that right.

Martyr to Public Liberty

Elijah Parish Lovejoy (1802–1837)

From a Silhouette of Elijah Parish Lovejoy

Eᴀʀʟʏ sᴜᴍᴍᴇʀ, 1827, and a young country fellow not long out of college heads westward to seek his fortune, like hundreds of other young men from the Eastern states. He dreams of making his place in life in Illinois, perhaps even as far west as the great Mississippi. He walks along the dusty roads, gladly accepting free rides and meals and lodging and doing small jobs for pay. The going is slow until a small loan from his college president in Waterville, Maine, speeds him on, so that eventually, in the fall, Elijah Lovejoy arrives in St. Louis, Missouri.

Sprawled along the great river, the thriving young city lay at the western edge of the East, the eastern edge of the West, the southern tip of the North, and the northern tip of the South. Young Lovejoy had never imagined anything like its bustling waterfront, its blocks of business buildings, its quick-moving citizens. All were different from the slow-paced Maine countryside of his youth. A man could grow up with this city; contribute something to it; make himself felt! With Eastern culture obviously in short supply, here was a place where he — Elijah Lovejoy — could put to good use his college education, his brief teaching experience, his wide background of reading, and his home religious training.

He paid little attention to the drunken rowdies outside the waterfront saloons, the frontiersmen fresh from Western Indian land, the voluble French moved up from downriver, or the barefooted Negroes, slave and free, running errands about the muddy streets. The world of the mind held more interest for young Lovejoy than the vibrant, colorful scenes of the lively city. He quickly attached himself to the small community of Northerners, mostly Easterners-lately-come-West. They, he wrote his God-fearing parents back in Maine, were the "most orderly, the most intelligent, and the most valuable part of the community."

With their help Lovejoy opened a school that winter — a private academy for young people of high-school age. It prospered, and for two years he ran it and taught the familiar academic subjects — English literature, ancient history, Latin, and Greek. Then, flattered by the offer to use his flair for words as a political journalist, he sold the school and joined the staff of the *St. Louis Times*. In its pages he vigorously promoted Henry Clay's campaign for the presidency, and was greatly disappointed when Andrew Jackson won the election.

Before long Lovejoy was made a partner in the *Times* publishing enterprise. He wrote home happily that he was doing well and enjoying his work and life. He lived at the City Hotel, attended the First Presbyterian Church regularly, and went frequently to worthwhile lectures and meetings. The West, he declared, was certainly the land of opportunity!

The coming of a revivalist to the Presbyterian Church changed the picture abruptly. Influenced by him, and by his upbringing by a minister father and a pious mother, Elijah Lovejoy decided that he too was called to be a minister. Within two weeks he sold his share in the newspaper and started east to attend the theological seminary at Princeton, New Jersey.

It was midterm, but Lovejoy talked his way into the seminary and buckled down to his studies as if his life depended on it. He was nearly thirty, and he felt he had no time to lose. That summer of 1832, he visited his family for a few weeks, then hurried back to New Jersey to plunge again into heavy reading and study. By the next spring he had finished the three-year course and was licensed to preach. After a few weeks at Newport, Rhode Island, he went to the Spring Street Church in New York. But the East, even New York, seemed tame to Elijah Lovejoy after the West, and he longed to get back to St. Louis.

An offer to edit a weekly religious paper to go into Protestant homes in Missouri, Illinois, and other states of the "Far West" seemed to him the perfect answer. It would combine his journalistic experience, his religious training, and his natural inclinations. He accepted enthusiastically.

"They are impatiently calling me to the West, and to the West I must go," Elijah wrote his family. To add to his small, somewhat uncertain salary, he secured an appointment from the American Mission Society to conduct religious services and organize Bible societies in the outlying regions of St. Louis.

Lovejoy arrived in St. Louis in September 1833, and in late November the first issue of the *St. Louis Observer* appeared. The paper would be nonpolitical, its editor wrote; it would keep a calm detachment and would aim to interest, inform, and inspire its readers. Letters and brief articles would be welcome, so long as the writers used "moderate and decent manners." We shall "hear both sides and may the right win."

The *Observer* was the first paper of its kind west of Cincinnati. The well-written editorials were certainly nonpolitical, but as slavery became a grave national problem the paper took on a more controversial tone. Its editor tried hard to steer a middle course. He personally believed the abolitionists were extremists and that emancipation of the slaves should come about gradually, with the slaveholders in some manner compensated for their losses and the slaves educated so they would be able to make their own way as free men.

In the spring of 1835, Elijah met and married a girl in St. Charles, a town where he had gone to preach, a few miles outside of St. Louis. They established a little home in the city, disregarding the storm blowing up about them.

Feeling on the subject of slavery was growing intense all

over the country, and violence was increasing. Illegal posses hunted runaway slaves. Southern sympathizers persecuted persons with antislavery views. Riots, attacks on newspapers, mob disturbances were everyday occurrences. Proslavery men distorted Lovejoy's statements against lynching and other brutal acts outside the law. And when an editorial of his urged slaveholders to treat slaves like human beings, it drew such fire that a weak assistant in Lovejoy's absence promised there would be no further mention of slavery in the *Observer*.

Lovejoy returned to find the city "literally gone mad" on the slavery issue, and himself no longer a popular leading citizen but a suspect character. He refused to be intimidated. He repudiated his assistant's promise, in spite of a letter from some important citizens urging him to "pass over in silence everything connected with the subject of slavery." And he disregarded warnings of proslavery men to shut up or get out of town. An attack on the *Observer* office was prevented when the paper's sponsors announced that they would defend their property by force if necessary. And Lovejoy escaped being tarred and feathered by a rowdy mob one night only because he happened to take a different route home that evening.

Lovejoy's friend Edward Beecher, president of a newly established college in Jacksonville, Illinois, and brother of Henry Ward Beecher and Harriet Beecher Stowe, urged Lovejoy to "keep on the course." He was pleased when Lovejoy printed in the *Observer* a statement of the principles of the American Anti-Slavery Society, adding that he agreed with most of them.

The *Observer* sponsors now retracted their promise of complete editorial freedom. Lovejoy handed in his resignation and wrote in what he thought was the paper's last issue, "The truth is, my fellow citizens, if you give ground a single inch, there is no stopping place. I deem it, therefore, my duty to take my stand upon the Constitution. Here is firm ground — I feel it to be such. And I do most respectfully yet decidedly declare my fixed determination to maintain this ground."

Impressed by Lovejoy's statement, some men he did not even know offered their help in defending his civil rights and the freedom of the press. But the more timid *Observer* proprietors sold the paper to their chief creditor. He, in a surprise move, invited Lovejoy to resume editorship, though from an office across the river, in the free state of Illinois.

Lovejoy agreed. He visited different Illinois towns to find the best location and decided on Alton. His brother John had recently come West to work on the *Telegraph* there. Alton's business was booming, and the Alton Presbyterians and others told Lovejoy they would be glad to have the *Observer* locate in their town. But the violence in St. Louis had died down as quickly as it had flared up, so that it seemed safe for the *Observer* to continue to be published in the old office. Lovejoy still insisted on freedom of discussion and printed articles on all sides of many questions, but he was somewhat cautious on the slavery issue. Circulation increased; the paper was expanded; there were plans to enlarge the office. Lovejoy's reputation was growing; he was appointed moderator of the area Presbytery.

Then Lovejoy reported in the *Observer* a particularly horrible mob burning of a Negro which had occurred in St. Louis, hitting out at the mobsters and at the unscrupulous judge who defended them. This stirred things up again, and once more Lovejoy was warned that his life was in danger and that he should stay off the streets. A mob broke into the *Observer* office and destroyed much of its equipment.

Lovejoy agreed that the time had come to move the paper to Alton. He sent his wife with their infant son to St. Charles while he arranged for the move. Ruffians broke up the Lovejoy furniture on the St. Louis dock, but somehow missed the *Observer* press. Unfortunately it reached Alton on a Sunday. Late that night as it stood on the dock waiting for delivery the next morning, proslavers from downriver broke it up and dumped the pieces into the Mississippi.

The citizens who had assured Lovejoy of his welcome to Alton were embarrassed. They held a public meeting to protest the destruction of the press and subscribed the cost of a new one. At this meeting they invited Mr. Lovejoy to tell them of his plans for the paper and to state his position on the slavery question.

After thanking the citizens for their generous promise to replace the press, Elijah Lovejoy spoke of his hopes to make the *Observer* an influential paper which would add its share to Alton's prestige and prosperity. Then he spoke of slavery. He was definitely against it, he said, though he was not an abolitionist. He thought there would be less need for the *Observer* to discuss this subject in the free state of Illinois than in the slaveholding state of Missouri. "But, gentlemen," he concluded, "as long as I am an American citizen, and as long as American blood runs in these veins, I shall hold myself at liberty to speak, to write and to publish whatever I please on any subject, being amenable to the laws of my country for the same."

The crowd applauded. They passed a resolution welcom-

ing the *Observer* to Alton and they authorized Elijah Lovejoy to order another press from Cincinnati. Then they
ended the meeting by enthusiastically pledging their loyalty
to the glorious Constitution and its Bill of Rights. Their
liberal attitude, they felt, showed Alton to be clearly supe-
rior to its commercial rival, St. Louis!

Lovejoy rented an office for the paper and bought a
small white house on the road leading to Upper Alton,
where he soon became minister of the new Presbyterian
Church. For a while, in order to pay his debts and get new
equipment for the paper and new furniture for his home,
Lovejoy also sold harness and clothing for an Alton mer-
chant. Along with this and planning the paper, gathering
news, attending meetings, preaching, and writing, he still
found time to take an active part in the life of the community. He started a lyceum in Upper Alton for lectures and
debates. His reputation as a speaker and writer grew. So did
the circulation of the *Observer*, which now had correspon-
dents and representatives in half a dozen states.

The antislavery people of the North and East wanted the
Observer to become a strong antislavery influence in the
frontier states; its Southern subscribers disagreed. All admitted that the paper's articles on world events and history,
its church news, stories for young people, and humorous
bits made good reading. There was not much about slavery,
but mob rule was often denounced. "We distinctly avow it
as our settled purpose," Lovejoy wrote, "never while life
lasts to yield to this new system of attempting to destroy by
means of mob violence the rights of conscience, the freedom of opinion and of the press."

As Lovejoy saw and heard and read more about slavery,

his feeling against it grew stronger. He called a meeting of the backers of the paper to tell them that he had become very nearly an abolitionist and to ask them if they wanted him to resign. They considered the matter, then directed him, "Follow the dictates of your own judgment. Write what you believe."

In the spring of 1837, Alton's trade suddenly dropped off. The land-speculation bubble burst, and people moved away. Some citizens suggested there might be a connection between the loss of the Southern river-trade and the *Observer's* remarks about slaveholders. They did not relish Lovejoy's suggestion that the Alton depression might be largely due to a greedy, materialistic outlook. They asked one another if he had not promised in his first public speech in Alton not to discuss slavery in his paper, and if he had not broken that promise.

When Lovejoy set up a meeting to organize an anti-slavery association in Alton, notices protesting the meeting were posted all about town, and a public gathering was called by "Friends of the *Observer* dissatisfied with its course." They passed a resolution urging its editor to stop his unwise agitation of the slavery issue. Lovejoy printed the resolution in the *Observer,* along with his answer — that he stood on his civil rights, and that he could not let others determine his editorial policy or limit his freedom of speech or the liberty of the press. The *Observer,* he wrote, was open to discussion on both sides of the question.

The new antislavery organization was formed, and the *Observer* continued to grow. Lovejoy, busy with his many duties, disregarded Alton's growing coolness toward him.

A secret society, led by two young Southern doctors,

undertook to get Lovejoy out of Alton. One dark night some of its members followed him, intending to scare him out of town by tarring and feathering him. When the men surrounded him, Lovejoy did not run or resist but said calmly that if one of them would deliver the medicine he was taking home to his wife, he would go with them peacefully. The mob leaders, impressed by his fearlessness, let him go. But that same night they entered the *Observer* office and broke up the press.

Lovejoy's supporters, and most Alton citizens, were angered by this act. How could they persuade Easterners to settle in Alton, which they pictured as a peaceable, orderly community, if this sort of news got out? The *Observer,* they declared, must remain in Alton. The *Alton Telegraph* offered its presses to print an extra issue of the *Observer* — an appeal for funds to purchase a new press. In it Lovejoy wrote, "Let the experiment be fairly tried whether the liberty of speech and of the press is to be enjoyed in Illinois or not." Money poured in, and soon the third *Observer* press was purchased in Cincinnati and shipped to Alton.

It was stored briefly in a warehouse, under a guard authorized by Alton's young mayor. Late one evening a small "orderly mob" arrived, handkerchiefs over faces, found the crated press, and proceeded to pry the crate open. The guard slipped away and informed the mayor, who rushed to the warehouse and ordered the men to leave. "We'll go as soon as we are through with our job," they told him defiantly. They rolled the press across to the dock, smashed it into bits, and dumped the parts into the river.

The next day the *Alton Telegraph* reported the event. In no uncertain terms its editor was warned that if there were any more harsh words about those who "think fit to stop the course of abolition in this place," the *Telegraph* press would follow the *Observer's* into the river. The *Telegraph* courageously retaliated by printing a series of letters showing Alton's loss of prestige in the East. One letter stated that people were being warned not to settle in a place where citizens trampled civil rights under foot. Another asked, "Has it become treason for an American citizen to publish his views on a matter which interests him as an American citizen?"

Again Lovejoy offered to resign, and again his resignation was refused, though this time not unanimously. Opinion in Alton was sharply divided. Many believed that only a small element was against the paper. Others thought it would be wise to move its office away. Quincy, Illinois, had guaranteed the *Observer* full protection if it chose to locate there. But Elijah Lovejoy reasoned that if lawless persons could drive the paper from one city they could drive it from another. He recalled what he had said in St. Louis: "If you give ground a single inch, there is no stopping place."

On a visit with his wife to her family in St. Charles, Lovejoy was upset when, after preaching at an evening church service, a mob followed him home and he had to escape by a back way. After their return to Alton, his wife collapsed. A third Lovejoy brother had come to Alton, and the three brothers kept all-night guard with loaded muskets, fearing that some of the St. Charles mob had followed the couple to Alton. Badly shaken, Elijah Lovejoy wondered if he had the right to subject his wife to this sort of thing. Yet to deny the right of free speech would be to violate every fiber of his being.

The regional antislavery society was to meet in Upper Alton, and President Beecher insisted that the meetings be open to "all friends of free inquiry." His idea was to bring in neutrals who might be influenced by the antislavery speeches, but his plan did not work. Instead, Beecher's invitation opened the doors to proslavery fanatics who disrupted the meetings with their questions, arguments, and objections. At length the antislavery people were forced to adjourn to a private home where they went on with their meeting under police protection. They accomplished two things — they formed a state society, and they resolved that the *Observer* must not retreat before illegal violence. "The cause of human rights, the liberty of speech and of the press imperatively demands that the press of the Alton *Observer* be reestablished at Alton with its present editor."

The young mayor, eager to restore the good name of his city, readily promised protection for a new press. On that promise, and with considerable financial manipulation and sacrifice, a fourth press was ordered for the *Observer*.

Dr. Beecher stayed on in Alton after the antislavery meeting, hoping to influence its citizens. In a public gathering he declared "that the free communication of thoughts and opinions is one of the inviolable rights of man and that every citizen may freely speak, write and publish on any subject, being responsible for the abuse of the liberty; that the abuse of this right is the only legal ground for restraining its use; that the question of abuse must be decided solely by a regular civil court and in accordance with the law, and not by an irresponsible and unorganized portion of the community, be it great or small."

Many Alton citizens disliked the connection he made

between law and order and freedom of speech and the press — especially freedom to express views they disagreed with. Why should one young editor upset the peace of a whole city by stubbornly insisting on his constitutional right to free speech? Let him go away and practice his free speech somewhere else!

At a second public gathering Elijah Lovejoy spoke. Standing straight and calm and grave, with "a spirit of cool determination," he said quietly, "I know that I have the right to speak and publish my sentiments, subject only to the laws of the land for the abuse of that right." The question was, would Alton citizens protect him in the exercise of that right? Very simply he told of the outrages he had suffered, the threats he had received, his wife's loss of health and peace of mind. He said he had thought of resigning and had agonizingly come to the decision that he must not do so in fear or at the demand of the mob. This, he said, was a matter of principle, a choice between law enforcement and mob control. For himself, he was determined to continue on his course "if need be until death."

The hall was silent as Elijah Lovejoy walked slowly out, and the eyes of many, even among his enemies, were wet. The opposition started a series of speeches in an attempt to wipe out the effects of his speech, but about sixty men had been so stirred by it that they organized themselves into an armed company pledged to defend the new press and its editor. The mayor not only sanctioned the company but agreed to be its honorary captain.

The arrival time of the press was a well-kept secret. It reached Alton in the middle of the night, was unloaded without mishap, and carried to a stone warehouse on the waterfront. The next evening the armed company, now formally organized under state law as militia, met at the warehouse. No trouble developed, so in the late evening most of them went home. Fourteen men, including the owner of the warehouse and Elijah Lovejoy, volunteered to stay through the night.

In the saloons along the waterfront troublemakers were gathering. Around midnight about thirty of them, armed with guns and pistols, stones and clubs, moved toward the warehouse.

"What do you want?" its owner asked the mob from an upper window.

"The press!" they shouted.

"No," the owner told them. "I am responsible for it, and my friends and I are determined to protect it, even at the cost of our lives."

"And we are determined to destroy it, even at the cost of ours," the leaders of the mob shouted back.

Stones flew, breaking windows, and a gun or two went off. From inside someone fired a shot, hoping to scare off the mob. It killed a man. This sobered the troublemakers and many of them left, but in a short while they came back, with more men and more guns. The mayor arrived and tried to break up the riot. When he saw that this was impossible, he went into the warehouse and begged the men there to give up. They would not. A church bell began to ring frantically. It brought out spectators, but no reenforcements for the men inside the warehouse.

"Surrender or we'll burn you out!" the mob leaders shouted. They lashed two ladders together and started a young fellow up them with a pail of flaming pitch to pour onto the wooden roof.

The defenders of the press knew that this must be stopped at all costs. Two volunteers slipped out and cautiously crept around the corner of the building. Before they could point their guns at the man on the ladder they were shot down. One was wounded only slightly; the other — Elijah Lovejoy — fatally. Hit by five bullets, he pulled himself up one flight of stairs, staggered into the counting room, and fell. Within minutes he was dead.

Silently the defenders slipped out of the building and headed homeward, except for one man who stayed beside the body of the young editor. The mob rushed into the warehouse and up the stairs. They pounced upon the press, hauled it to an opening, and pushed it out. With a thud it landed on the dock below. Rushing down, the men completed its destruction.

The next day Elijah Lovejoy was quietly buried. It was his thirty-fifth birthday. Although every effort was made to hush the matter, reports of the Alton riot spread like wildfire. All across the country there were protest meetings, addresses, sermons, newspaper editorials. Emerson, Channing, Horace Greeley, William Cullen Bryant, John Quincy Adams, and many others called Lovejoy "a martyr to public liberty." In Springfield, Abraham Lincoln spoke against mob outrages and men who were allowed to "throw printing presses into rivers and shoot editors."

Because of Elijah Lovejoy many men, among them Wendell Phillips, Owen Lovejoy, and John Brown, pledged their lives to the antislavery cause. Across the top of its stationery the American Anti-Slavery Press printed the words:

LOVEJOY THE FIRST MARTYR TO AMERICAN LIBERTY —
MURDERED FOR ASSERTING THE FREEDOM OF THE PRESS.
ALTON, NOV. 7, 1837.

He did not die in vain. Speaking at the centennial observance at Colby, Lovejoy's college, in 1937, Herbert Hoover
said, "Since his martyrdom, no man has openly challenged
free speech and free press in America."

We should be eternally vigilant against attempts to check the expression of opinions that we loathe.

The Great Dissenter

Oliver Wendell Holmes, Jr.
(1841–1935)

T HE YOUNG lieutenant-colonel in the Union Army informed his father that he intended to study law at Harvard Law School. "A lawyer can't be a great man," Oliver Wendell Holmes, Sr., told his tall son scornfully.

Until that moment Holmes, Jr., had not been absolutely sure that he wanted to study law. He had been looking for something that would take his mind off the three years of horror he had been through in camps and on battlefields, off thoughts of friends dead and dying, off his own upset nerves and physical suffering from wounds in chest, neck, and heel. He wanted to use his mind, use it to the hilt, stretch it as far as it would go. Three years earlier, before he put on a uniform, he had written in the Harvard graduating class book, "If I survive the war, I expect to study law as my profession, or at least for a starting point."

Now his father's attitude made him stubbornly determined. He was not committing himself to the law for life merely by taking a law course at Harvard. Besides, he did not much value the advice of his father, who enjoyed writing silly ditties or sentimental articles for the new *Atlantic Monthly* more than working in his own field of medicine.

But Dr. Holmes had reasons for his low opinion of law in general and of the Harvard Law School in particular. There were many more poor lawyers than good ones around. All the law most of them knew was what they had learned from a couple of years' reading of English law books in some lawyer's office in preparation for the superficial oral examination for admittance to the bar. Harvard Law School offered little more, with its three elderly professors expounding the law in long dull lectures.

Young Holmes, crossing the Charles River to Cambridge for his first class, resolved to get as much as possible out of the law school. He must make up the three years his war service had put him behind schedule in his professional education.

The newer method of arguing actual cases in class had not yet arrived at Harvard, but the law students had organized a club to discuss and try cases among themselves.

Holmes learned as much from this club, named for John Marshall, the great Supreme Court Justice, as from the lectures. He learned even more from the reading and research he did independently, and from long talks with brilliant fellow students he brought home for the evening. In his second year he spent three hours a day in a lawyer's office, where he helped prepare actual cases. The legal detail bored him, but he was interested and excited by the broader aspects of law. In its history he saw the moral development of mankind and the changing patterns of society. The law prized ideas above things; it called for one's best thinking, and kept one continually learning. Being a legal scholar appealed to him as a sort of perpetual intellectual adventure. He was sure now that law was not just a starting point but the right lifetime career for him. "A man can live greatly in the law," he was to write later, perhaps remembering and refuting his father's scornful statement.

Oliver Wendell Holmes, Jr., was twenty-five when he finished law school. After spending several months in England and on the Continent, he returned to read for the bar examination, which he passed in 1867. He took the natural next step of joining a Boston law firm, but his heart was not in it. Being a practicing lawyer did not interest him; his delight was in delving into the underlying principles of the law. He was pleased to be asked to bring up to date a standard legal reference book, *Kent's Commentaries on American Law*. He worked at it feverishly, trying in the two-year time allowed him to check and add all helpful cases, both English and American. Besides doing this, he wrote reviews and occasional articles for the *American Law Journal*.

Holmes, Jr., still lived at home. He had little money of his own, while his family had plenty and wanted him there. He felt close to his mother and enjoyed his younger brother and sister, but had no sense of comradeship with his father. Dr. Holmes's unconsciously condescending manner toward his children annoyed Oliver Wendell, Jr. And being spoken of only as his father's son hurt his sense of self-esteem.

Partly for financial reasons and partly because he was so taken up with his law work, young Holmes was thirty-one before he married. The girl was Fanny Dixwell, a charming, congenial companion whom he had known all his life. For a time they lived in the Holmes family home; then they took a little apartment, where they were as happy as two youngsters released from school.

Law scholars began to take notice of Holmes's brilliant writing and of his masterly revision of Kent, and he was invited to teach constitutional law at Harvard. He was a natural teacher; his comments were wise, lively, and to the point. Holmes's students began to see law as an exciting, growing thing related to life and its changing conditions. By using actual cases in class, much as the old John Marshall Club had done, he encouraged the students to think. "It is revolting," he said, "to have no better reason for a rule of law than that it was laid down in the time of Henry IV. It is still more revolting if the grounds upon which it was laid down have vanished long since, and the rule simply persists from blind imitation of the past."

In 1880, Holmes was invited to give a series of lectures on common law at the Lowell Institute. Could he make the subject interesting to a general audience? he wondered aloud to Fanny. And what about his neck? His neck? she asked. Smiling a little wryly, he told his wife of his father's remark that he never could be a lecturer because his neck was too long. Fanny just threw back her head and laughed. Then, for hour after hour, evening after evening, she sat by, needlework in hand, as her husband worked on the lectures.

They were a huge success. By dividing the subject into types of problems, translating legal terms into everyday language, and illustrating general principles with dozens of homely examples, Holmes made common law not only understandable but interesting to his intelligent but legally untrained audience. He hardly ever looked at his notes, but talked directly to his listeners almost as if he were telling a small group some entertaining story. If his neck was long, no one seemed to notice it!

The next year, close to Holmes's fortieth birthday, the lectures were published in book form. *The Common Law* was highly praised in both England and America; it was called a "notable work" which put a "solid foundation under American law." It did more than that; it marked a new approach to law and a break with the old idea that law was something that had been set forth once and for all. Holmes maintained that law changed as it was affected by the "felt necessities of the time" and even by the prejudices of judges. The book's very beginning — "The life of the law has not been logic; it has been experience" — made traditional lawyers sit up and take notice.

The Common Law placed Holmes squarely among top-flight legal thinkers and writers. Harvard's President Eliot made him a full professor of law at Harvard Law School. Dr. Eliot assumed he would be there for the rest of his life; members of the Harvard faculty seldom left. But only three months after beginning work Holmes was invited to be-

come an Associate Justice on the Massachusetts Supreme
Court. It was a hard decision for him to make. He liked
teaching and considered it highly important work. He enjoyed the association with the other professors, especially
with a young lecturer named Louis Brandeis, whose alert
mind was akin to his own, and he delighted in his contacts
with the students. But being on the bench would bring him
into the active currents of life and give him a chance "to
understand and interpret the New America that was growing up."

America was indeed growing up. Agricultural regions
were changing over to industry; women were emerging
from the home; labor was becoming powerful; big business
was growing bigger. And these "felt necessities of the time"
were having an influence on the law.

Professor Holmes became Justice Holmes, accepting the
offer which he called "a stroke of lightning which changed
all the course of my life." The youngest of the seven judges
on the bench, he lacked judicial experience, but this was
more than balanced by his quick mind, his capacity for
attentive listening, and especially by his ability to go to the
heart of a matter. "The point of contact," he said, "is the
formula; the place where the boy got his fingers pinched;
the rest of the machinery doesn't matter."

To Sir Frederick Pollock, an English legal friend,
Holmes wrote, "Well, I like my work far more than I
dreamed beforehand. The experience is most varied — very
different from that one gets at the bar. . . . One sees, too,
a good deal of human nature, and I find that I am interested
all the time."

For twenty years Oliver Wendell Holmes, Jr., sat on the

highest court of his native state, the last three years as Chief Justice. His quick mind, philosophic approach, and common-sense judgments stimulated the other judges to keener thinking. He was independent and high-minded in his interpretation of the law, uninterested in politics, uninfluenced by personal prejudice. Individual liberties were important to him, and he placed human rights above property rights, no matter who was concerned, in a day when this was unusual. As he made law vital in a new sort of way, his influence and reputation grew. Yale, and later Harvard, made him a Doctor of Laws.

In 1902, Holmes wrote to Sir Frederick, "If I haven't done my share in the way of putting in new and remodeling old thought for the last twenty years, then I delude myself." It was no delusion.

That year President Theodore Roosevelt appointed Oliver Wendell Holmes (no longer Junior, since his father had died) to serve on the highest court in the land. If leaving the Harvard professorship for the Massachusetts Supreme Court was a "stroke of lightning" which changed his ways, the transfer to the Supreme Court of the United States was a much sharper stroke. It meant leaving the city and state which had been his home for sixty-one years, and where most of his friends and associations were.

"Shall we go?" he asked Fanny.

"Yes," she answered without hesitation. "It will be a great adventure for you." For herself, she dreaded the social life it would involve, not foreseeing the popularity her kind nature, brilliant mind, and keen wit would bring her in Washington.

The judge admitted that the idea of this "adventure into

the unknown" brought him "a mighty joy." It would be exciting "to have the chance to do one's share in shaping the laws of the whole country."

So the Holmeses cut the ties with the past and moved to the nation's capital, and Holmes wrote to Pollock, "Yes, here I am — and more absorbed, interested, and impressed than ever I had dreamed I might be. The work of the past seems like a finished book, locked up far away, and a new and solemn volume opens. The variety and novelty to me of the questions, the remote spaces from which they come, the amount of work they require, all help the effect."

Applications poured in from lower courts all over the country for cases to be heard by the Supreme Court — cases of state *vs.* federal Government, individual *vs.* state, and individual *vs.* federal Government. Holmes viewed the justices' guide — the Constitution of the United States — as the "means of ordering the life of a progressive people" and "a frame of government for men of opposing opinions, and for the future." Unlike some of the justices, he felt that the Constitution was intended to "keep step with the march of the age," and should not hamper social or economic experimentation.

President Roosevelt, striking out against large business combinations, was angry that his new justice from Massachusetts voted against the majority of the Court when it declared a certain big-business merger illegal. Bigness in itself, said Holmes, was not a crime, and combinations were the natural result of free competition in a growing society. They were as much the right of the employed as of employers, he said, and so were strikes and picketing (without violence), although he personally did not approve of them.

Because of his independent viewpoint, Justice Holmes came to be known as the Great Dissenter. It was not the number of times that he voted against a majority opinion of the Court that gave him this name, so much as the importance of the issues when he disagreed, and the strength and eloquence of his dissenting argument.

Justice Holmes especially valued the First Amendment's guarantee of freedom of speech and of the press. "If there is any principle of the Constitution that more imperatively calls for attachment than any other," he wrote, "it is the principle of free thought — not free thought for those who agree with us but freedom for the thought that we hate." To a friend he complained, "Free speech means to most people, you may say anything that I don't think shocking." No one, he felt, had a corner on absolute truth; there should be a "free trade in ideas," so that society would not be deprived of the wisdom that ideas might contribute. "The best test of truth," he wrote, "is the power of the thought to get itself accepted in the competition of the market."

When the First World War came, Justice Holmes recognized that the security of the country required placing limits on freedom of speech. "War opens dangers that do not exist at other times," he said. And he reminded people that "the most stringent protection of free speech would not protect a man in falsely shouting fire in a theater and creating a panic." But Holmes was not swept away in the hysterical fear that overtook many Americans, even some in high places. "I think," he said, "that we should be eternally vigilant against attempts to check the expression of opinions that we loathe and believe to be fraught with death, unless they so imminently threaten interference with the lawful and pressing purposes of the law that an immediate check is required to save the country."

The Espionage Act, passed by Congress in 1917 to prevent disloyalty in the Army or Navy and attempts to obstruct recruiting, seemed to Holmes too severe. He thought that most of those affected were not criminals but "little people caught in the meshes of a war hysteria." But he went along with his associates in deciding against three defendants accused under that act, in the Schenck, Frohwerk, and Debs cases, and in each of them it was Holmes, the champion of free speech, who wrote the Court's opinion denying the appeal.

Justice Holmes felt differently when the repression of free speech continued after the war was over. "It is only the present danger of immediate evil or an intent to bring it about that warrants Congress in setting a limit to the expression of opinion," he said, and in several cases involving freedom of expression he dissented from his "brethren." He was usually supported by Justice Brandeis, his old Harvard friend, who was now a member of the Court and whose liberal thinking often ran parallel to his own, sometimes even outstripping it.

The most famous Holmes dissent came in the Abrams case. A few Russian-born persons had printed circulars protesting the sending of American troops into Russia after the 1917 Russian Revolution. Holmes called this a weak endeavor to defeat a military effort but not a plan to overthrow the Government. His dissent was a passionate and eloquent defense of free speech. In it he set up a test to resolve the conflict between necessary governmental restraint and the protection of free speech which the Constitution guaranteed. The test was: Did the words used produce "a clear and present danger" that would result in evils the country might constitutionally seek to prevent? If so, and only if so, did the Government have the right to overrule the First Amendment.

Holmes's Abrams dissent was called a "landmark of noble courage" in an "era of hysteria," and his "clear and present danger" test became a yardstick in future trials. Although nearly eighty, the Justice was still a fighter, with a "wallop in either fist." Freedom of expression called out the most powerful "wallops" of this man who was, as his friend and later Justice Felix Frankfurter said, "committed to the fullest freedom of the mind." Justice Holmes felt strongly that Americans needed to be reminded of the importance of the First Amendment. "We have grown so accustomed to the enjoyments of these rights," he wrote a friend, "that we forget they had to be fought for and may have to be fought for again."

Each Supreme Court Justice was allowed a secretary. Justice Holmes had his selected for him from the graduating class at Harvard Law School — a new one every year. "Holmes's Annuals," they came to be called. The Justice and his wife treated these young men like the sons they did not have, and the secretaries adored both of them. Justice Holmes listened to them, argued with them, treated them as equals. They gained more than they gave, for Holmes looked up most of his law references himself and wrote out his opinions in longhand. All was not work. He delighted in showing the successive young men his favorite haunts near the capital, driving along the Potomac, across to Arlington, and in the spring discovering or rediscovering beautiful bowers of cherry blossoms, magnolias, and dogwood. On his eightieth birthday Mrs. Holmes gathered as many of the old secretaries as could get to Washington for a surprise dinner for the Justice. And what a celebration it was!

Fun-loving and always "inescapably young," the Justice had a real genius for friendship. He took especial delight in young people and they in him. For he gave them the best of himself, tried open-mindedly to understand them, and thoroughly enjoyed "the clash of contending views."

Each summer the Holmeses went up to the old family seaside place north of Boston. In the first years the Justice did a good deal of walking, even some bicycling. Later he settled down to spending most of his time in all kinds of reading, in writing letters, and in visiting with friends. Always, too, he had his share of the Justices' summer job of passing on hundreds of applications for hearings by the Supreme Court.

Justice Holmes's physical vitality outlasted that of his wife, who died at eighty-eight. She had brought poetry into his life for sixty years, the Justice said as he went bravely on with his work. His mind was as alert as ever, even when his strength of body waned and he drove instead of walking, with his current secretary, the two miles each way to the Capitol for the Court sessions. Every year the rumor went out that Justice Holmes was retiring. And every year the Justice squelched the rumor. "Work," he said, "is never done while the power to work remains." The truth was that he loved his work. "The rule of joy and the law of duty," he wrote a friend, "seem to me all one."

On his ninetieth birthday there was a nationwide salute

on the radio to "one who finds in the law a constant adventure," with tributes from the most important persons of the legal world. "We honor him," said Chief Justice Hughes, "but what is more, we love him." Justice Holmes listened, then made a moving though brief response, for "to express one's feelings as the end draws near is too intimate a task."

He was the oldest Justice ever to serve on the Supreme Court of the United States. Resigning at ninety-two, he reluctantly admitted, "My energy gives out." From then on he rested more, drove, read a great deal, and had many callers. His conversation was still brilliant. Chief Justice Hughes called him "the best company in Washington," and his young English friend and correspondent Harold Laski testified, "None of us who love him feels that he is old, only that he is more experienced than we are."

Two days before his ninety-fourth birthday, Justice Oliver Wendell Holmes died. By virtue of his service in the Union Army more than seventy years before, he was buried in the National Cemetery at Arlington. He had left an indelible mark on American judicial life, especially in the area of individual freedoms, and had richly fulfilled his "trembling hope that somehow the world will be a little better for our striving."

Freedom to Read

The American Library Association
(founded 1876)

SOMETIMES an organized group can champion a particular freedom better than an individual. For many years the American Library Association, as the authorized spokesman of the public libraries of the country, has stood up in defense of the "freedom to read." This is in keeping with the aims of this oldest and largest national library association in the world — "to make books and ideas vital forces in American life, to make libraries easily accessible to all people . . ."

It seems strange that anyone in a democracy should oppose the freedom to read and the freedom of inquiry. Yet some overzealous citizens actually try to prevent libraries from making available to the public books and other materials which contain ideas they disapprove of. These voluntary censors have complete confidence in themselves as judges of what is true or false, good or bad, helpful or harmful. They are certain that nothing they read could hurt *them*, but they are not so sure about others. They do not stop with trying to persuade other people to think the way they do; they actually attempt to control others' thinking by limiting what they read.

Closing off any paths to knowledge weakens the nation as well as its individual citizens. "In a democracy with our traditions," says Dr. James Conant, noted American educator, "only those reasoned convictions which emerge from diversity of opinion can lead to the unity and national solidarity so essential for the welfare of our country." Certainly independent thought has contributed so many rich and varied ideas to our American society that the nation is justified in having confidence in its citizens' ability to do their own investigating and draw their own conclusions.

President Johnson has called books and ideas the most effective weapons against ignorance and intolerance, which he terms two of the worst enemies of a democracy. And he says, "The library is the best training ground for enlightenment that rational man has ever conceived."

To provide this enlightenment, libraries must represent as many subjects as possible impartially and from many angles. Expert selection from the mass of available materials requires balancing community needs with budget limitations. If librarians listened to the voices of any single set of people in making their selection they might well shackle the free-wheeling, naturally curious American mind, which is the country's greatest resource.

Fear lies behind most movements to curtail the freedom to read. People feel especially insecure in times of war, hot or cold. Besides the fear of foes outside the country, they fear disloyalty within. Some fearful people begin to suspect unfamiliar ideas and become afraid to tolerate opinions which are different from their own. Instead of encouraging open discussion they try to shut off access to ideas they dislike. They overlook the fact that curtailing the expression or availability of ideas limits the freedoms pledged in the First Amendment. And they totally disregard Yale's late President A. Whitney Griswold's words: "Books won't stay banned. They won't burn. Ideas won't go to jail. In the long run of history the censor and the inquisitor have always lost. The only sure weapon against bad ideas is better ideas."

American librarians have felt a deep sense of responsibility to defend people's freedom to read. As community leaders they have courageously insisted on making and keeping books and ideas "vital forces in American life."

At the 1938 conference of the American Library Association a representative group of public librarians passed a resolution pledging themselves to be on guard against the growth of censorship and bias in book selection in libraries. "Such practice," they declared, "is foreign to American democratic ideals." Later that year the Council of the ALA, its governing body, went on record in these words:

"The library recognizes no censorship except the community's own standards of good taste. It cherishes the right and welcomes the duty to supply its readers with books on all sides of controversial questions."

The next year, when feeling was high against the Germans, a book importer reported receiving threatening letters because he was supplying libraries with German publications. An American Library Association committee reassured him and others with the statement: "Librarians, officially, can have only one position when it comes to anything that concerns the interchange of ideas. We believe and maintain that our collections of books should represent all shades of opinion, in so far as that is possible. The public deserves to have complete information on all subjects. There is no strength in ignorance."

At its 1939 conference, the American Library Association issued a document termed the Library's Bill of Rights, and recommended that it be adopted by individual library boards throughout the country. This is the way it read:

Today indications in many parts of the world point to growing intolerance, suppression of free speech, and censorship, affecting the rights of minorities and individuals. Mindful of this, the Council of the American Library Association publicly affirms its belief in the following basic policies which should govern the services of free public libraries:

1. Books and other reading matter selected for purchase from the public funds should be chosen because of value and interest to people of the community, and in no case should the selection be influenced by the

race or nationality or the political or religious views of the writers. [In 1944, this sentence was added here: "Further, books believed to be factually correct should not be banned or removed from the library simply because they are disapproved by some persons."]

2. As far as available material permits, all sides of questions on which differences of opinion exist should be represented fairly and adequately in the books and other reading matter purchased for public use.

3. The library as an institution to educate for democratic living should especially welcome the use of its meeting rooms for socially useful and cultural activities and the discussion of current public questions. Library meeting rooms should be available on equal terms to all groups in the community regardless of their beliefs or affiliations.

In commenting on this Library's Bill of Rights, the ALA's executive secretary said, "Whether we have the courage and the ability to live by that creed may now be tested." And indeed it was. As the Second World War came closer, the passion for voluntary censorship spread like a prairie fire. In scores of communities eager citizens tried to take over the librarian's job of book selection, confident that they knew exactly how it should be done. Their enthusiasm waned somewhat during the war years, then became strong again around the midcentury mark.

Some of the voluntary book censors were most concerned with protecting the morals of the young. They thought that young people should not be exposed to the ideas or language of Joyce, Steinbeck, Thomas Wolfe, Pearl

Buck, and other modern writers. They asked librarians to remove these books from library shelves. Some even wanted to throw out Hawthorne, Whitman, Shakespeare, and the Greek myths. An English teachers' organization in denouncing such censorship said, "The more the choice is narrowed, the less education remains." Almost without exception librarians stood firmly on their pledge to supply the public with representative books of accepted literary merit.

Voluntary reading censors with strong feelings against minority groups wanted to ban from public libraries pro-Negro, and sometimes pro-Jewish, books. This effort, too, was successfully combatted by librarians in almost every state.

The most difficult type of censorship for librarians to fight was — and still is — in the area broadly termed political. In the early fifties, when fear of communism was at its peak, determined individuals and narrowly nationalistic groups made valiant efforts to keep out of libraries books by authors suspected of having Communistic leanings, and also books about communism or the Soviet countries. Many of these earnest censors — especially in California and Texas but in other states too — really believed it would help keep America strong to remove from library shelves all books favoring the United Nations and civil liberties.

Imagine the courage it took for a librarian in a small town, perhaps after ignoring threatening letters and anonymously prepared lists of "unacceptable" authors, to stand up to a delegation of townspeople calling on him or her to try to dictate the book-selection policies of the library. The beginning was usually the demand for the removal of certain controversial books from the library shelves. The assailed librarian found strength in the Library's Bill of Rights, in state library association Committees of Intellectual Freedom, and almost always in the backing of the local board of trustees. The requirement that requests must be in written form and signed helped turn away many such attacks, as did the use of diplomacy and soft words of reason.

Not all librarians had this sort of dedicated, determined courage. A few agreed to the demands made on them and so weakened the community book collection. Others put controversial books in locked cabinets or piled them in back rooms. Incredibly, a few public book-burnings actually took place. Even worse, perhaps, was the undermining of timid librarians' self-confidence until their book orders included only "safe" books with little solid meat for inquiring minds to feed on.

But timid librarians were very much in the minority. Most librarians met censorship attacks head-on and, as agents of the whole community, fought for the public's right to read and to have available worthwhile material of all shades of opinion. Here and there a librarian was abused in the press, and a few actually lost their positions for resisting censorship demands. But many, many more — though often at the expense of gray hairs — achieved deepened character and reputation by bravely standing up for the freedom-to-read principle. "No group in America steadily, quietly, and successfully resisted all pressure of bigotry and censorship more than the library profession," said Luther Evans, then Librarian of Congress.

The American Library Association had gone beyond the

Bill of Rights initiative in creating a Committee on Intellectual Freedom "to recommend such steps as may be necessary to safeguard the rights of library users in accordance with the Bill of Rights of the United States and the Library's Bill of Rights." And in 1948 two more paragraphs were added to the Bill of Rights:

> Censorship of books, urged or practiced by volunteer arbiters of morals or political opinion or by organizations that would establish a coercive concept of Americanism, must be challenged by libraries in maintenance of their responsibility to provide public information and enlightenment through the printed word.
>
> Libraries should enlist the cooperation of allied groups in the fields of science, of education, and of book publishing in resisting all abridgement of the free access to ideas and full freedom of expression that are the tradition and heritage of Americans.

A note also was added to the effect that not only books but "all materials and media of communication used or collected by libraries" were covered in the Library's Bill of Rights. And in 1961, this sentence was added: "The rights of an individual to the use of the library should not be denied or abridged because of his race, religion, national origin, or political views."

Some inventive souls promoted the idea of labeling library books on communism or by Communist sympathizers. After studying a report by the Committee on Intellectual Freedom, the ALA Council stated that labeling was a censor's tool, an attempt to prejudice the reader, a violation of the Library's Bill of Rights, and inconsistent with democratic principles. Moreover, it would be impossible to find any person or group of persons capable of impartial labeling.

Other professions — educational, legal, journalistic — came to the support of the library's effort to prevent limitation of free inquiry. A Yale professor lamented the fact that Americans could "fail to recognize that ideas are subject to diversity of interpretation," and a Princeton professor said, "The library is the citadel of the free spirit. It is today imperiled." From the American Bar Association came the statement: "Any fear that our people have become so soft-headed that they must be protected against an opportunity to examine the books of authors whose personal views or conduct are obnoxious is unfounded." A Midwestern newspaper editor stated, "Public libraries are the institution most vital to the preservation of free speech and freedom of thought in the country."

In May 1953, a group of publishers and librarians met in Westchester, New York, and worked out a Freedom to Read statement. Its seven points were: that it was in the public interest to make available the widest possible choice of reading; that publishers and librarians did not necessarily endorse the ideas in the books they chose; that books were not selected on the basis of the authors' beliefs; that existing laws were depended upon to deal with problems of obscenity in books; that prejudging books by labeling them was not in the public interest; that it was the duty of publishers and librarians as guardians of the people's freedom to read to resist encroachments on that freedom; and, finally, that

publishers and librarians, believing that suppression of
ideas is fatal to a democratic society, should assume a
positive role in providing good books to take the place of
bad ones, thus staking out "a lofty claim to the value of
books."

The 1953 American Library Association conference,
held in a California stronghold of extremism, was full of
tension. At a dramatic moment an open letter from President Eisenhower to the ALA president bolstered the dedication of the librarians at the conference and those at home
to the principle of freedom to read.

"Our libraries," wrote President Eisenhower, "serve the
precious liberties of our nation: freedom of inquiry, freedom of the spoken and the written word, freedom of exchange of ideas. Upon these clear principles, democracy
depends for its very life, for they are the greatest sources of
knowledge and enlightenment. And knowledge — full,
unfettered knowledge of its own heritage, of freedom's
enemies, of the whole world of men and ideas — this
knowledge is a free people's surest strength. . . . The
libraries of America are and must ever remain the homes of
free, inquiring minds. To them, our citizens — of all ages
and races, of all creeds and political persuasions — must
ever be able to turn with clear confidence that there they
can freely seek the whole truth, unwarped by fashion and
uncompromised by expediency."

The President's letter made front-page news all across the
country and helped turn the tide against the persecution of
free inquiry. It also gave librarians, as one of them said,
"cause to feel proud of belonging to a profession whose
leaders have dared to stand up against the tyranny of

thought control in an era of witch-hunting and book-
burning."

Gradually most of the people of America became supporters of — or at least reconciled to — the principle of
free access to ideas. They came to see that stifling others'
points of view was no way to protect or promote their own,
and that obstructing the flow of ideas contradicted the
whole fabric of the American democratic way of life. In the
1960's many of those energetic individuals and groups who
in the 1950's sought to impose their points of view on
communities by emotional appeal, by threats, and by devi-
ous methods, were beginning to recognize that the strength
of a democracy lies in its diversity, and to agree with
librarians that the inquiring mind is something to be encouraged, not suppressed.

As the 1960's wore on, American librarians reported
that the American reading public was showing increasing
interest in getting more than one point of view on controversial subjects. Despite television, people were reading more and were ranging over wider fields in their reading. For this changed — and changing — atmosphere,
great credit goes to the American Library Association and
its members for continuously and courageously champion-
ing the American heritage of freedom to read.

II

THE SECOND IS
FREEDOM OF EVERY PERSON
TO WORSHIP GOD
IN HIS OWN WAY

*Only on the grounds of tolerance for all religious opinions, and
for none, can true religion itself flourish.* CECIL NORTHCOTT

RELIGION *played an important part in the colonizing of
America. Most of the settlers came from a background of religious opposition and persecution. In America, the colonists
happily followed their own way of worship and, accustomed as
they had been to a single, state-sanctioned faith, saw no reason
for tolerating any other.*

*"Religious freedom," the Italian statesman Luigi Luzzatti
wrote, "is the most difficult and slowest of liberties to root itself
in private life and in the life of the state." It took time and exposure to different varieties of faith and the courage of many
liberal-minded men and women to change American colonists
into tolerant, live-and-let-live human beings. Over the years in
America, as Milton Konvitz wrote in his* Fundamental Liberties
of a Free People, *"Religious persecution gave way to religious
exclusion; exclusion gave way to reluctant toleration; toleration
gave way to religious freedom; religious freedom developed into
separation of church and state."*

*By the time the colonists threw off England's shackles and
created their new nation, most of them were convinced of the
justice and wisdom of religious freedom and of the separation
of church and state. Their leaders committed themselves and
their descendants to these, both in the national Constitution and
in every state Constitution. In the new United States all religious
bodies were equal before the law, and the word "heresy" fell out
of use. This "radical experiment" was the new nation's con-
tribution to the progress of civilization.*

*Religious freedom, like the other freedoms, needs cherishing.
In today's world it still requires careful and courageous tending,
even as it did in the days of Roger Williams, Thomas Jefferson,
and its other champions, great and small.*

No man should be bound to worship or maintain a worship against his own will.

A Livelie Experiment

Roger Williams *(1603–1683)*

THE HANDSOME young clergyman and his attractive wife moved toward the welcoming crowd on the Boston shore unsteadily, after nearly ten weeks fighting the winter seas on the small ship *Lyon*. Governor Winthrop welcomed them warmly. "You have come at a most opportune time, Mr. Williams," he said. "When you are rested, the elders want to talk with you about replacing the assistant minister in our Boston church; he is returning to England on the *Lyon*."

The elders were impressed with the young minister's quick mind, his learning, and his strong religious feeling. Unanimously they invited him to fill the vacancy in their church. Then Mr. Williams asked them a few questions. Had they broken completely with the established Church of England? Did they permit full freedom of conscience? And was there separation of religious and civil authority in the Massachusetts Bay Colony?

When the elders answered all three questions in the negative, Roger Williams told them courteously but firmly that he must refuse their offer. He was sadly disappointed he said, to find even less religious freedom in the New World than in the Old.

The elders were angered at the young man's boldness, but they held their peace, remembering that Mr. Williams was said to have important Puritan friends in England and that Governor Winthrop seemed disposed to be friendly toward him. Time might soften the upstart's radical views and show him the wisdom of conforming to the ways of the colony.

But Roger Williams did not change his views; he did not conform to the ways of the Massachusetts Bay Colony; and he did not hesitate to speak his mind freely — a habit which the elders and magistrates found more than a little disturbing. After getting acquainted with the town and the outlying settlements, he visited the distant Indian camps and made a start at learning their language, so he could do missionary work and also trade with them. His father had been a London merchant-tailor, and in spite of his years as a student at Charterhouse and Cambridge and as a minister in Essex, young Williams had not forgotten the business principles he had learned in his boyhood.

That spring of 1631, only two months after his arrival, Roger Williams was invited to become assistant to the elderly minister in the more liberal church at nearby Salem. For a short time he and his wife lived in Salem. Then a journey to the south convinced Williams that they would be better off in the Plymouth Colony. It was much more to his liking than the church-governed Bay Colony, and it would be easier to make a living there farming, fishing, and trading with the Indians.

In Plymouth Colony the Williamses were welcomed and provided with shelter and farmland. Although Mr. Williams held no office in the church he preached often and, according to Plymouth's Governor Bradford, the teaching of this "godly and zealous" man was "well approved." Williams soon was able to converse with the Indians, having a natural flair for languages and, as he said, "the painful, patient spirit to lodge in their filthy smoky holes to gain their tongue." He also learned their customs and ways of thinking, became friends with their important chiefs, Massasoit and Canonicus, and started a profitable trading business with them.

Roger Williams believed that the white men should pay the natives for the lands they took over. This idea disturbed Governor Bradford, for the Pilgrims had never paid the Indians a penny. He asked Mr. Williams to write out his thoughts on the subject.

More disturbing to Elder Brewster and other Plymouth church leaders were Roger Williams's religious views. His outspoken opinions brought on so much controversy in the church that they were not sorry when, after two years in Plymouth, Mr. Williams decided to accept a call to return to the Salem church. A few neighbors volunteered to go with the couple and their baby girl, born shortly before they left.

The leaders of the Massachusetts Bay Colony were not pleased to learn that the disturbing Roger Williams had returned to Salem. Governor Bradford had shown his paper on the matter of the land belonging to the Indians to Governor Winthrop, who in turn had shown it to members of his Council. They called Williams before them to account for it, claiming it cast doubt on his loyalty to the Crown, since it was the King who had given them their land. Williams told them that they might burn the paper, which he had written privately for the Governor of Plymouth, and he declared his loyalty to the King, so the Council decided to let the matter pass. Everyone knew that discovery constituted ownership, that there was plenty of land left for the natives, and that if Englishmen had any duty at all to the Indians it was not to pay them but to convert them! But the Council determined to be on guard for the next disrupting idea this firebrand Williams might have.

About this time two capable Puritan ministers, Thomas Hooker and John Cotton, arrived in Boston. Cotton especially was critical of Williams, disapproving of his stand on the separation of church and state, on paying the Indians, and on "soul freedom." He could not understand why Williams objected to compulsory church attendance or why he found oath-taking out of place in civil courts because of its being a religious gesture. Or why, when the ministers of the colony were asked to work out a religious doctrine to which everyone should be ordered to subscribe, Williams should oppose it as an attempt to "rule the soul." Mr. Cotton, asked by the Council to reason with Mr. Williams, admitted that he "could not shatter the rocky flintness of his [Williams's] self confidence."

At every turn Williams's strong feeling for spiritual freedom conflicted not only with John Cotton's more rigid beliefs but with the very foundations of the church-governed Massachusetts Bay Colony. His belief that government should have no authority in religious matters, and that magistrates should not have power to punish religious offenses, seemed like anarchy to the colony leaders. Time and again Williams had to interrupt his parish work or drop his hoe or fishpole or cancel a trading expedition to go to Boston to be reproved by them. At last the irritated magistrates put him on probation for a year. They also put pressure on the Salem church to get rid of its "unruly Teacher" by letting it be known that Salem's use of Marblehead Point for pastureland, controlled by the Massachusetts court, depended on Roger Williams's dismissal. The Salem church at last was "dragooned into submission," and Mr. Williams withdrew.

With the help of a family legacy the Williamses had bought a house in Salem, hoping to make it their permanent home. But on one of his trading trips Roger Williams had taken the precaution to make a verbal agreement with Chief Canonicus to secure a strip of land in the Narragansett country.

Before his year of probation was up, Williams was called before the full Bay Colony court to be tried for having "broached and divulged divers new and dangerous opinions." Four were named: that the natives were the true owners of the land; that oaths should not be taken as part of civil procedures; that membership in the Parish Assembly in

England was unlawful; and that "civil magistrates' power extended only to the Bodies and Goods and outward state of men." Roger Williams agreed that he did indeed hold these "dangerous opinions."

He made his defense in Thomas Hooker's dirt-floored church in Newtown, later Cambridge. Eloquently, courageously, he attempted to combat the bigotry of his age and of the Bay Colony. "Your breath blows out the candle of liberty in this land," he told them, but to no avail. The court passed its sentence — within six weeks he must leave the colony. Generous-hearted Williams told his wife Mary not to grieve; "some fifty good men did what they thought was just."

Friends won a petition to grant a stay until spring, but when it was reported that Williams had persuaded others to his opinions and might take them with him into exile, the court resolved in January to rid itself at once of this "symbol of dissent." A ship was in Boston harbor, ready to leave for England; they determined that Williams should sail on it, and they summoned him to Boston to inform him. Williams, ill with a fever, sent a doctor's certificate stating that he was unable to travel, but the court was not to be thwarted. It sent a pinnace to Salem with fourteen men armed and with orders to get Williams and put him aboard the England-bound ship. A storm delayed the pinnace, giving former Governor John Winthrop and his son time to send Williams a warning. These good friends of his — in spite of different religious viewpoints — urged him to go at once to his Indian friends in the Narragansett Bay region.

Williams hurriedly sold his trading post, mortgaged his house, arranged for the care of his wife, two-year-old Mary and the three-month-old baby named Freeborn, and set out, ill though he was, in the winter storm. When the armed men arrived, they found that their man had been gone three days — where, no one could tell them.

In bitter cold the sick, lonely, discredited man made the "sorrowful winter's flight" through wild country, over snow-covered forest trails, across icy rivers and creeks, resting briefly in sheltered nooks, fighting for survival against heavy odds. Probably about the fourth day he reached Massasoit's winter camp. There Indian friends welcomed him, fed and lodged him, and through the winter nursed him back to health. Williams in turn did them a service by arbitrating a difference that arose between Massasoit and Canonicus.

Early that spring Roger Williams and companions who had joined him began to cut down trees and build shelters on a nearby spot. But Edward Winslow, now Plymouth's Governor, sent a kindly warning that this land was within the jurisdiction of Plymouth Colony, which was "loath to displease the Bay" by harboring its exiles. If Mr. Williams would but move across the river he would be in free country and, added Governor Winslow, "we should be loving neighbors together."

Williams understood the problem well. He and his six companions scouted about until they found an ideal place for a settlement. It was in Narragansett territory, between two rivers, near a spring, with fine farming land and pasture for cattle, a good harbor, and waters teeming with fish. When Williams tried to buy the land, Canonicus insisted that he had already paid for it in service. Much later Roger Williams wrote, "It was not price nor money that could

have purchased Rhode Island. Rhode Island was purchased
by love."

Williams named the settlement Providence and planned
it to be "a shelter for persons distressed from conscience."
Letters from the Winthrops and from Sir Harry Vane, the
friendly new Governor of the Bay Colony, informed him
that his wife was well, and encouraged him to persevere in
setting up a settlement based on his principles of liberty of
conscience, separation of church and state, and the fundamental rights of man.

Axes rang as trees were cut and cabins built. Williams's
house was made large enough to hold religious and civic
meetings in and to entertain groups of visiting Indians or
Englishmen. The settlers plowed and planted, fished and
hunted. Williams checked with the Governors of Plymouth,
Massachusetts, and the newly established Connecticut colonies to make certain the land was free from all English
claims. He visited Indians for miles around, preaching,
making treaties of friendship, and setting up a trading
business with them and with the Dutch and English.

That summer of 1636, Mary Williams came to Providence with her two small daughters and several Salem
families. Twelve ten-acre lots running from river to hilltop
were laid out, and the heads of the first twelve families
signed a simple agreement. It was unlike any in history, for
it provided for complete separation of religious and civil
affairs and allowed "full liberty for each to walk his own
path to God." For, said Roger Williams, "Forced worship
stincks in God's nostrils." In the presence of the settlers and
many Indians he signed a written deed to the land; then
Canonicus put on it his mark of a bow and his nephew his
mark of an arrow.

Time after time Roger Williams interrupted his work to make peace between tribes and between Indians and English. He wrote truly that he spared not "purse nor pains nor hazards very many times that the whole land, English and Native, might sleep in peace, securely." His peacemaking attempts succeeded because he and the Indians could "speak understandingly with each other, the nations much loving and respecting him for his love and council." At the risk of his life he tried to prevent the fierce Pequots from making war, and he informed his persecutors, the Massachusetts Bay Colony, of the murderous plans of the Pequots and their chief, King Philip. Even after English troops massacred most of the Pequot tribe, he managed almost singlehandedly to hold down major Indian threats to English settlers for nearly forty years, when the settlers' stupidity and greed brought on King Philip's War.

The Providence colony grew steadily and prospered, to the great displeasure of the Massachusetts Bay Colony. One of their settlers wrote home, "Mr. Roger Williams is the man of greatest power in all of New England. A thinker and scholar of learning is he, and a good trader and influence with the Indians. Massachusetts fears him, for he is now a great landowner, doubtless the greatest in any of these parts."

Many emigrants from England chose to settle in Providence. So did outcasts from the Bay Colony and from other colonies, and some of them made a good deal of trouble for Williams and his colony.

The Massachusetts Bay, Plymouth, Connecticut, and New Haven colonies had joined together in a defensive union they called the New England Confederation. They deliberately left out Roger Williams's settlement because they said it was unauthorized by the King and its laws were too permissive. But they coveted, and began to claim, some of its territory. Clearly the Providence Plantations needed an English charter as well as its deeds of purchase from the Indians.

And so in 1643, Roger Williams went to England to get a charter for his colony. He had to sail from New Netherlands, since he was not allowed in Boston. While waiting for a ship, he advised the Dutch Governor on how to end the serious trouble he was having with the Long Island Indians. On shipboard Williams wrote a useful book about the Indians, *Key to the Language of America*. It contained not only translations of phrases and key words but information on Indian culture and customs. Published in London, this little book established Roger Williams as an authority on the American Indian.

In England a bitter war was going on between King Charles I and the Parliament. The Massachusetts Bay Colony used its English agents to thwart Williams's efforts to get a charter. In spite of this, within a few months he obtained from Parliament a liberal charter which covered both Providence Plantations on the mainland and "Road" Island. It contained everything Williams asked for — freedom of conscience and of worship, rule by common consent, separation of religious and civil affairs. The Parliament Commission hoped that this "livelie experiment" would not have undue influence in England!

John Cotton had published in London his arguments against Williams's religious doctrines, as justification for Williams being banished from the Bay Colony. Just before he left England, Williams published an answer. He called his pamphlet *The Bloudy Tenent of Persecution for the Cause of Conscience* and in it he stated clearly and forcefully his views on religious freedom, separation of church and state, and consent of the governed. These were no longer mere theories as they had been when John Cotton attacked them. Now they had a firm basis in fact in Williams's colony. The ideas expressed in *The Bloudy Tenent* were revolutionary for that age: "Persecution of men's bodies seldom or never do their souls any good." . . . "No man should be bound to worship or maintain a worship against his own will." . . . "Magistrates can have no more power than the common consent of the People shall betrust them with." So startling was this pamphlet that Parliament ordered it burned. But before that happened, it had been widely read — and Williams was safely aboard a ship bound for America, carrying his precious charter.

He carried, too, a letter from Parliament ordering the Massachusetts Bay leaders to give him safe passage through their colony and urging them to be more friendly with Mr. Williams and his colony, which was now to be known as Rhode Island. The Bay Colony leaders could not deny Williams safe passage, but they were so soured at his success in getting the charter and so firm in their belief in a church-controlled state that they continued to be his enemy.

His own people welcomed him with affection and honor. Fourteen crowded canoes waited where the overland trail from Boston met the river to escort him to Providence. There he greeted his family and the infant son he had not seen and set to work to put into action the provisions of the charter which recognized Rhode Island as an independent colony.

It took Williams three years to overcome the objections of the four separate towns of the colony — Providence and Warwick on the mainland, Portsmouth and Newport on the island — to a union with central government, and to work out fair distinctions between central and local courts, laws, and administration. By 1647, all the towns agreed to subscribe to the Constitution of Rhode Island — the first democratic commonwealth anywhere in the world.

Besides acting as peacemaker with the Indians, Williams also had to earn a living for his family. He set up a trading post near Warwick, twenty miles away, where Dutch and English ships could easily stop, and spent about half his time there. Trading, preaching, teaching, helping the Indians, and trying to keep peace made Roger Williams gray-haired before his time. But his mind never grew old, nor did his belief in religious liberty ever grow dim, or his love for human beings lose its warmth.

In 1651, Roger Williams had to go to England again, because the Massachusetts Bay Colony, the Plymouth Colony, and the Connecticut Colony all were pressing their claims to Rhode Island territory. This time John Clarke, the Newport minister, went with him. The Bay Colony grudgingly granted them permission to sail from Boston. Some of their friends held high posts in Oliver Cromwell's Government, now in power. But the other colonies also had powerful friends, and they opposed Williams's and Clarke's every move. The Council granted Rhode Island Colony permission to continue under its 1644 charter, but a new charter was needed. While waiting for it, Williams wrote several small books and had them published. When it became clear that the waiting might go on for years, Williams left the task to Clarke and returned to Providence. He took back instructions to neighboring colonies to allow their people liberty of conscience and to stop molesting the Rhode Island Colony, but the colonies paid no attention to them.

At Roger Williams's suggestion, the Rhode Island towns established an Assembly made up of six representatives from each town. As its first president, he set up courts, fixed official wages, and smoothed out difficulties. After his term was over he held other offices and helped in whatever way he could, at the same time working as trader, farmer, preacher, and peacemaker.

Unlike other colonies, Rhode Island welcomed Jews. Enough Jews settled in Newport to establish there, in 1658, the first synagogue in America. Rhode Island also welcomed Baptists and Quakers, who were persecuted elsewhere. When other colonies demanded that Rhode Island expel their Quakers, they were told in no uncertain terms that this colony had no law against any form of worship, and that all were welcome, whatever their belief, so long as they did not threaten the civil order.

After twelve long years in England, John Clarke returned in 1663, bearing the new charter, signed by Charles II. It was the first to separate religious and civil authority and to permit "full libertie in religious concernments," guaranteeing its citizens that "all men may walk as their consciences persuade them, everyone in the name of God." The Rhode Island charter, said Roger Williams happily as he set about transcribing it, provided "such peace, such security, such liberties for Soule and Body as were never enjoyed by any English men, nor any in the world I yet have heard of." So broad and satisfactory were its provisions that it served as the state's Constitution for nearly two hundred years.

Roger Williams's efforts to stave off the bloody King Philip's War might have succeeded but for the rashness, injustice, and greed of the other colonies. When the Indians fell upon the whites in all southern New England in 1675, Williams, though seventy-two, became captain of the Providence militia. He drilled soldiers for the defense of the town, but he firmly refused to join the English in any offensive warfare against the natives. After the settlers had slaughtered hundreds of Narragansetts, the Indians retaliated by killing and burning on the Rhode Island mainland. While most of the settlers fled to the islands, Roger Williams and twenty-six other men remained in Providence to defend it. As seventy Indian warriors descended upon it, Williams hobbled out to meet them. He tried to get them to turn back, but they continued to advance, though assuring Williams of his personal safety.

After King Philip's death, the war ended, the settlers returned, and Roger Williams helped rebuild Providence. He became its town clerk and remained active in town affairs until his death at eighty.

To Roger Williams, courageous, selfless, dedicated, this nation owes much. His "dangerous ideas" that government should be the servant rather than the master of the people, and that citizens should have full liberty in matters of conscience and in civil affairs so far as consistent with the good of all, provided the basis for much of the American Constitution. "He had influenced the life and thought of two continents," wrote James Ernst. "His Providence experiment had weathered every storm. Religious and civil liberty and the rights of man had for the first time been made a part of constitutional law and government."

> [No Christian shall] *bee any wares troubled . . . in respeck of his or her religion.* <small>MARYLAND TOLERATION ACT</small>

A Place of Refuge

The Lords Baltimore:
George Calvert (1580–1632)
Cecilius Calvert (1606–1675)
Charles Calvert (1637–1715)

'he LORDS BALTIMORE

George Calvert	Cecilius Calvert	Charles Calvert

IN THE EARLY 1600's nearly everyone in England was interested in the New World. It had timber and furs and fish, tawny natives to trade with, and fertile farmlands to colonize. Poor men saw there a new place to try their luck; rich men, new ways to increase their fortunes. For a share in the profits the King gladly granted land and trading privileges, and many companies were formed for ventures in the Western world.

George Calvert, a Yorkshireman of good family, educated at Oxford and widely traveled in Europe, was a member of the Virginia Company. He was also on the council of the New England Company, and he owned a tract of land in Newfoundland. Calvert had advanced rapidly at court; he was an assistant to Sir Robert Cecil, the secretary of state and trusted councilor to King James I; and the King had given him lands in Ireland for his services in investigating complaints there, and had knighted him. When Cecil died, King James made Calvert his secretary of state. It was no easy matter to represent the King's interests in an unfriendly Parliament. Sir George Calvert took the responsibility seriously and performed the difficult task well.

Suddenly Sir George resigned his post, announcing to the Protestant King and Parliament that he had become a Catholic. King James, instead of punishing or fining him, as he might have done, allowed Sir George to sell his office for a handsome sum and to keep his lands in Ireland. In addition, as a sign of his favor, the King made him Baron of Baltimore in the Kingdom of Ireland.

A Roman Catholic in a violently Protestant England, and with no place at court, Lord Baltimore was at loose ends. For several years there had been a small fishing settlement on his Newfoundland property. Now he decided to develop this settlement and make it into a place of refuge for persecuted Catholics or any who suffered because of his religion. He sailed for Newfoundland in the fall of 1627, leaving his family in Ireland, and spent several weeks supervising the building of fisheries, storehouses, and homes. The next spring he returned to Newfoundland with his family and forty colonists, intending to settle there permanently. But it was a disheartening experience. That summer six French privateers attacked the fisheries. Lord Baltimore was able, with the help of his men, to capture them, but he could not conquer the rugged Northern climate. When the short summer season gave way to grim winter, it brought chills and sickness and misery to the Calverts and other colonists.

After much thought, Lord Baltimore decided to write off his Newfoundland investment as a loss and to leave the settlement to the hardy fishermen. He would petition the King for a land grant far to the south, perhaps within the bounds of warm and sunny Virginia, and establish a colony there.

He sent his wife and children to Virginia while he explored the coast. The Virginia Colony objected to Calvert's settling to the south of the James River, so he sought a similar grant to the north. The Virginians were members of the established Church of England and strongly anti-Catholic. They had no liking for the Catholic nobleman's idea of setting up a colony anywhere nearby. But Lord Baltimore, having made up his mind that the land bordering the Chesapeake Bay was exactly the right place for his colony, went back to England to petition the new King Charles I for a charter to establish a colony "founded on religious freedom, where there would not only be a good life, but also a prosperous one, for those bold enough to take the risk."

Charles I granted Lord Baltimore's petition; he even let him draw up the charter himself. His territory lay to the north of the Potomac River and to the south of the fortieth parallel. As proprietor, Lord Baltimore would be its complete master, required only to see that its laws were "agreeable to reason and to the laws of England," and to pay as rent to the King two Indian arrows, to be delivered at Windsor on the Tuesday of each Easter week, and a fifth of any gold and silver which might be found. The King named the new colony Maryland, in honor of his queen, Henrietta Maria.

Lady Baltimore with several of the children sailed for England to be with her husband while he was shaping plans for the new colony, but their vessel was lost in a storm. Of his large family, Lord Baltimore had left only the two oldest sons. In his grief he plunged into work on the details of the charter. When all was in order and waiting only for the King's great seal to be affixed, Lord Baltimore himself suddenly died. His title, and the Maryland charter, came to his eldest son, Cecilius.

Like his father, Cecilius (named for Sir Robert Cecil) was an ardent Catholic. He was also a tolerant man, who wanted others to enjoy the same freedom of belief he desired for himself. He had sympathized with his father's idea of establishing a colony where not only Catholics but everyone might worship as they chose. Now the second Lord Baltimore resolved to turn his father's dream into a reality.

As soon as the charter had the great seal affixed, with Cecilius's name substituted for Sir George's as proprietor, a proclamation invited adventurers to share in the settlement of the new Maryland colony. The settlers' passage money would entitle them to a certain amount of land, for which they would pay the proprietor a yearly rental. They must take with them personal and household essentials, tools, and seeds. All Christians, both Catholics and Protestants, would have freedom of religious belief and worship.

Cecilius knew, as his father had known, that if there were to be enough settlers for the colony to prosper, Protestants must be included as well as Catholics. Many Catholics belonged to old, wealthy families; they would prefer to continue being fined for their religion at home than to share the hard life of pioneering colonists. And the King, besides being a Protestant, wanted the colony to be a commercial success, like Cecilius.

In spite of some Protestant opposition to the venture because of its Catholic proprietor, more than two hundred passengers sailed out on the *Ark* and the smaller *Dove* in November 1633. Cecilius and his young wife wanted to go, but he felt he must remain in England to settle many problems connected with setting up the colony. He sent his brother Leonard to be the first resident Governor of Maryland, giving him detailed instructions. He was to be "very careful to preserve unity and peace amongst all the passengers on Shipp-board . . . and treat the Protestants with as much mildness and favor as Justice will permit. And this to be observed on Land as well as at Sea." In the New World the colonists were to establish friendly relations with the natives, plant crops, build houses, a fort, and a church.

The little *Dove* was mourned as lost in a storm, but she turned up again in the Caribbean, to the joy of all. In those islands fresh water was taken on, and more provisions, and seeds. The ships also stopped at Point Comfort to deliver a letter from the King to the Virginia Governor. He was courteous but cool, since he regarded these newcomers as intruders, for Maryland seemed to him a natural extension of Virginia soil.

Father White, a Jesuit priest who came over with Governor Calvert, wrote an account of the sailing of the *Ark* and the *Dove* up the beautiful Chesapeake Bay. He told of Indians along the shore disappearing as the ships approached, and of anchoring off a sheltered island to plant a cross as they took over the land in the names of Charles I and Lord Baltimore.

A friendly captain who acted as guide and Indian interpreter helped the Governor make friends with the natives. They were not at all hostile, and their chief gave Governor Calvert permission to "sit down wherever you please in my land." With Father White's help, the colonists and Indians became true friends. They even lived together in the little Indian village until the settlers built their own houses in their newly founded town of St. Mary's.

It was not the Indians but a Virginian, William Clayborne, who made trouble for the new colony. Several years earlier Clayborne had set up a trading post on Kent Island in Chesapeake Bay, right in the heart of the Maryland territory. He refused to acknowledge Governor Calvert's authority, there were "incidents," and finally an armed battle, which Clayborne lost. He left the region, but returned later to take his revenge.

When the *Ark* left for England that first year, it took a load of beaver furs, some Indian baskets, wampum, and arrowheads, and a good report of the colony's beginnings. Catholics and Protestants were living together harmoniously, "side by side on terms of equality." At the altar of Father White's Catholic chapel, where Catholic settlers worshiped, Governor Calvert swore to uphold his father's ideals of religious liberty. He invited Protestants of all varieties to come to Maryland, and they came in such numbers, both from other colonies and from England, that they soon greatly outnumbered the Catholics. Many Quakers and members of other new sects settled in Maryland. Nowhere else in colonial America, save only in Rhode Island, was so much freedom of conscience and worship allowed.

When the Indians who had been converted to Catholicism wanted to make Jesuit priests gifts of land, Lord Baltimore and Governor Calvert forbade it, and the Assembly of freemen, called by the Governor, agreed. It also ruled that no religious organization should have more land than just enough for its churchyard and burying ground, and that priests should be subject to the laws of the colony like any other settlers. Lord Baltimore's orders were that all religious groups should be on an equal footing.

The royal charter granted the proprietor alone the right to make the colony's laws, but the Assembly wanted to make its own laws. On his brother Leonard's advice, Lord Baltimore at last agreed, retaining the right of veto. Setting up the Assembly as a law-making body was a big step ahead in popular government. So also was the right to pay fines in tobacco!

Cecilius, Lord Baltimore, wanted very much to visit Maryland, but he was still too busy with the management of the colony's affairs in England. So Leonard went back to give his brother firsthand information about the colony — and a handful of its red earth. The priests, Leonard told Cecilius, had been so helpful in keeping the Indians friendly that Maryland had escaped the terrible wars that had gone on in other colonies. Better call the Fathers "Mister," Lord Baltimore advised, and not mention them in the reports sent back, for Catholics were very much out of favor in England, and the Protestants in Parliament might try to undo the good work done in Maryland if they thought that priests were responsible for any part of it.

Leonard had scarcely returned when the Maryland Puritans took advantage of Cromwell's Puritan Government in England. With the aid of a disguised pirate and the rebel-trader Clayborne, they overthrew the Calvert Government. They sent Father White to England in chains, burned Catholics' homes, and forced the St. Mary's townspeople to seek safety in their fort. Governor Calvert hurried to Virginia, where he hired soldiers to go back with him to drive the rebels out of St. Mary's and Clayborne off Kent Island, to which he had returned. That same year of 1647, Governor Leonard Calvert died. He had governed Maryland for thirteen years justly and ably, with not a single incident of persecution for religious belief.

In view of the Puritan Government in England and the strong Protestant majority in Maryland, Lord Baltimore replaced his brother with a Protestant Governor. But the times were uneasy, religious feeling was intense, and there was restlessness among members of all faiths in Maryland.

To provide "for the more quiett and peaceable government of the Provence, and the better to preserve mutuall love and amity among the Inhabitants," Lord Baltimore drafted an Act Concerning Religion. The Maryland Assembly passed this "Toleration Act" in 1649, but only after adding to it some intolerant provisions, most of which were never enforced. They introduced into Maryland to a slight degree the religious persecution from which it had previously been entirely free. Yet the Toleration Act, with its guarantee that no Christian should "bee any wares troubled . . . in respeck of his or her religion nor in the free exercise thereof," was a great forward step toward religious liberty.

The first Easter week after Charles II became King, Lord Baltimore himself took to Windsor the two Indian arrowheads required as rent in the Maryland charter. The next year, 1661, he appointed his only son Charles to be resident Governor of Maryland. Governor Charles Calvert and his bride were warmly welcomed there. They brought many servants and luxuries and there was much festivity, music, dining, and dancing in the Governor's mansion.

By now the Protestants in Maryland outnumbered the Catholics ten to one. Among them, coming mainly from Virginia, were many mischief-makers who did their best to end religious toleration. Charles Calvert thwarted them at every turn, insisting that every citizen of Maryland be able to "speak his beliefs without fear." He welcomed to the colony all people — "Dutch, Italian, French, Catholic, Jew, Indian, Negro, rich or poor" — and even sponsored the passage of a liberal naturalization law for their benefit.

There were many disputes over the Pennsylvania, Delaware, and Virginia boundaries. Governor Calvert tried to settle them by negotiation, but several times he led out armed forces to resist what he felt were encroachments on his territory. Never, he prided himself, did Maryland lose land to rival colonies. Trouble with the hostile Susquehanna Indians, too, he met firmly. Though he was accused of being high-handed, tactless, and impulsive, and of trying to exert undue influence on the Assembly, he always had the good of the colony at heart. When he took his family to England for a visit, in 1669, he could report to Lord Baltimore that the colony had grown, that it enjoyed comparative calm, and that it was prosperous, thanks chiefly to its main crop, tobacco.

Cecilius Calvert, the second Lord Baltimore, died in 1675. A gentle, unselfish, just man, he had carried out his father's ideals for religious freedom in his colony as successfully as was possible under the conditions of the time. For forty years he had worked for the interests of Maryland, though never once had he stepped foot in it.

Governor Charles Calvert was now the third Lord Baltimore and proprietor of the Maryland colony. He went at once to England to settle his father's affairs and assume his title. The next year, while still in England, he was called before the King's Privy Council for questioning in regard to the petition the Anglicans in Maryland had sent to the Archbishop of Canterbury that the Church of England be made the established church of Maryland. Lord Baltimore told the councilors that it would not be possible to set up a single state church in the colony, because more than three fourths of its people were not Anglicans but "dissenters." Though the idea persisted, Lord Baltimore continued to oppose it, backed by Catholics, Quakers, and non-Anglican Protestants.

Charles Calvert returned to the colony in 1680. He remained four years, then went again to England. Times were uncertain. Five years later the Protestant Revolution broke out, and when Protestant William and Mary were placed on the throne, Lord Baltimore's proprietary rights were taken from him, because of his Catholic faith. In 1692, Maryland was made a royal province, and a succession of royal Governors succeeded the Calverts. Lord Baltimore's petition to have the province restored to him was refused on the grounds of his religion.

Ten years later the Anglicans succeeded in making the Church of England the established church of Maryland. On gaining control, they denied liberty both to Catholics and to non-Anglican Protestants. They moved the seat of the Government from the old Catholic center at St. Mary's to the active Protestant center of Annapolis. The so-called "penal period" began for Catholics, causing many of them to move to Pennsylvania.

Religious tolerance in Maryland was at an end. No longer was the colony a "land of sanctuary," where a man could "live in peace, free to worship as he pleased." But in later years men and women of Maryland would be proud to claim citizenship in a state which, as a colony, was founded and maintained by a liberal, tolerant family of Catholic noblemen who did their utmost to carry out their ideals of freedom of religious belief and worship.

I owe my conscience to no mortal man.

A Free Colony for All Mankind

William Penn (1644–1718)

IT TOOK MORE than a moment of glory experienced at twelve to turn William Penn into a Quaker. More, too, than being moved by a sermon from the lips of the Quaker preacher Thomas Loe. After all, William Penn was the son of an admiral of the English fleet, known to the King. He was headed for a brilliant career in the law or at court, while the Quakers, or "Friends of the Truth," were a peculiar new sect, despised both by Catholics and by Protestants.

A sensitive, serious-minded youth, William was impressed by the Quakers' simple faith, with its emphasis on spiritual things, and by their courage when persecuted for their beliefs. During his college years at Oxford he refused to go to chapel and he met often with a nonconformist group. For this, the authorities fined him, and his father lectured him. When he did not change his ways, he was expelled from Oxford and reasoned with, thrashed, and driven from home by his father. Then the admiral father, relenting, packed his stubborn son off on a Grand Tour of Europe "in company with several persons of rank." Unfamiliar scenes, he hoped, would cure William of his foolish notions.

The plan almost succeeded. In Paris William fenced so well that, when forced to draw his sword because he had carelessly failed to return a stranger's salute, he sent the man's sword flying from his hand. Instead of killing him, as custom required, Penn let the stranger go. He doubted, he said later, "if the whole ceremony were worth the life of a man."

At a Huguenot college he attended lectures which strengthened his ideas on religious liberty, on peace among nations, on simpler forms of worship, and on a morality based on man's natural goodness. Then, after nearly two years abroad, William Penn returned to England "a most modish Person," according to the Penns' gossipy neighbor Pepys. He entered the school of law at Lincoln's Inn in the year of London's Great Plague. The horrible sights he saw depressed him and filled him with a sense of life's insecurity.

Admiral Penn had a large estate in Ireland. He decided that managing it would occupy his son's mind and also test his legal and business ability. And he hoped, too, that William might find the viceroy's brilliant court at Dublin to his liking.

Young Penn did his father's task well. He put things in order on the estate and got on well both with tenants and court nobles. He rode a good deal and formed a taste for country life which he never lost. The experience of helping put down a mutiny of the troops at Carrickfergus fortress made him consider a military career — and have his portrait painted in a suit of armor.

Then, in Cork, William Penn again encountered Thomas Loe, the Quaker preacher, and found in his teaching the faith he had been seeking. He began to attend Quaker meetings and to spend much time with members of this new sect. He still dressed in cavalier ruffles and carried a sword, and he frequently forgot the Friends' peculiar customs, such as leaving on their hats and addressing everyone by the singular *thee* and *thou*. Once, when a soldier interrupted a Friends' meeting, Penn seized him by the shoulders and started to throw him down the stairs. The Friends quickly reminded Penn that using violence was against their principles, but the angry soldier called in troops and had the Quakers carried off to jail. Penn, conspicuous among the soberly dressed Friends and recognized as the son of a large landowner, was offered his freedom. He would not leave; instead, he sat down and wrote so convincing a letter to the president of the province that it won the release of his friends and himself.

When Admiral Penn learned of his son's association with Quakers, he called him home. This time the breach between father and son seemed too wide to be healed. Unwelcome at home, Penn began traveling about England, talking at Friends' meetings and visiting the Quakers in prisons. He met their founder, George Fox, and the two men became lifelong friends.

Because of his father the admiral, Penn was known at court, and he often appeared there to seek pardon for imprisoned Quakers. To the courtiers' dismay, Penn refused, even in the presence of King Charles II, to take off the large cavalier hat he still wore, though with fewer fancy feathers. Fortunately the "Merry Monarch" treated this good-naturedly, and the story goes that when Penn approached Charles, hat on head, the King removed his own elaborately plumed hat. "Friend Charles," Penn is reported to have asked, "why dost thou uncover thyself?" To which the King is said to have answered, "Friend Penn, it is the custom of this place for only one person to remain covered."

Penn did not, however, adopt all of the Quaker peculiarities, especially those which made them seem conspicuous and unmannerly. His clothes were well tailored, his linen spotless, his manners courtly. "I know of no religion," he said, "which destroys courtesy, civility, and kindness."

Besides going to the court to use his royal favor to improve the Quakers' condition, Penn preached often and wrote a great deal about the Friends' beliefs. One of his pamphlets was printed without being formally licensed by the Bishop of London, England's official censor. The bishop declared it "blasphemous," and, since no author's name was shown, put the printer in jail. At this, Penn gave himself up, admitting that he had written the pamphlet. He expected to be fined; instead, he was thrown into the Tower of London, to remain there, the bishop said, until he took back his words. Courageously Penn declared, "My prison shall be my grave before I will budge one jot, for I owe my conscience to no mortal man." For this he was denied the favors of heat, exercise, and better food often given political prisoners, but he did not flinch. "Neither great nor good things are ever achieved without loss and hardships," he said, and he set to work writing the small book he called *No Cross, No Crown*. He also addressed — unsuccessfully — a "noble plea for religious toleration" to the Council, in which he reminded them that it was an Englishman's privilege to be tried before being condemned. After nine long months the admiral took pity on his son and by interceding with the King's brother, the Duke of York, won young Penn's release.

Admiral Penn decided that since his son's beliefs "had survived the test of imprisonment and disinheritance," they must be based on deep conviction. He acknowledged William as his son again and sent him back to Ireland to look after the family estate. Young Penn did this so well, along with freeing unjustly imprisoned Irish Quakers, that when he returned to England several months later the estate was in good shape and not a single Quaker remained in an Irish prison.

In this year of 1664, the Protestant Parliament passed the Conventicle Act, which prohibited the right of public worship to all sects except the established Church of England. Some sects met in secret, but the Quakers scorned to do this. Penn, preaching in front of a padlocked London meeting house, was arrested along with another Quaker. After two weeks in Newgate Prison, they were tried at the Old Bailey for disturbing the peace and inciting a riot. Penn was able, because of his legal training, to protest these accusations as false. This angered the judges, and they ordered the jury to find Penn and his companion guilty. Outraged, Penn jumped up and shouted to the jury, "Ye are Englishmen, mind your privileges; give not away your rights!"

"Stop his mouth!" a judge directed. "Jailor, bring fetters and stake him to the ground."

"Do your pleasure," Penn answered. "I matter not your fetters."

Again and again the jury, encouraged by Penn, returned the *not guilty* verdict. For this the members of the jury were fined, along with the prisoners, and all were sent to prison until the fines should be paid. "Illegal!" shouted Penn, and he demanded the liberty the jury's verdict had given him. No one listened, but later, when the jury brought suit for illegal imprisonment, a higher court acquitted it, declaring that no jury could be fined for its verdict. Penn, by his indignant protests, had advanced the cause of civil liberty in England.

This jail sentence was particularly hard for William Penn, because his father was dying and wanted his son with him. Over his objections, the admiral paid both his and his companion's fines. He also wrote his good friend the Duke of York of his illness and asked him to watch over William and, if necessary, to intercede for him with the King. Fully reconciled to his son's religion, Admiral Penn blessed him before dying.

After tending to his father's affairs, William Penn retired into the country to write and think — and to be near Guli Springett, a sweet-tempered, beautiful, and intelligent young Quaker woman with whom he was deeply in love. Along with other Quakers they saw George Fox off to America to establish Quaker meetings in Newport, Baltimore, and other colonial towns. Then Penn journeyed to northern England, and also across the channel to Holland, to preach and to organize Quaker groups.

William and Guli were married in 1672, when Charles II's Declaration of Indulgence had brought a measure of relief from religious persecution. But the Parliament claimed the King's act was meaningless without its approval. This Protestant Parliament waged a continuous battle with the King, who was sympathetic to Catholics. It tried to control him by limiting his money, which he must get through Parliament, but the extravagant King tricked it by secretly borrowing large sums from France's Louis XIV in return for a pledge to restore Catholicism in England and to help France fight the Protestants in Holland.

The persecution of the Quakers was soon worse than ever, with fines, property confiscations, banishment, imprisonment, even death. Penn used his friendship with the royal family to try to improve conditions. This was misunderstood by many, even the Quakers. When he asked for religious liberty for Catholics as well as for Protestants, some wondered if secretly he might not be a Catholic himself. Penn's only answer was his statement, "I abhor two Principles in Religion, and pity them that own them. The first is, Obedience upon Authority without Conviction; and the other, Destroying them that differ from me for God's sake."

When George Fox, back from America, was imprisoned for refusing to take the oath, which was against the Friends' belief, Penn went to court to ask the Duke of York to release Fox. The Duke welcomed Penn warmly and spoke up in favor of the Quakers and of religious freedom. But though Fox was released, not much else changed. Penn continued to write and to preach and organize Friends' meetings all over England. He also went with Fox and other Quaker leaders to Holland and Germany to strengthen the Friends' movement there.

Since George Fox's return from America, Quakers had talked about setting up a colony there as a refuge from England's harsh religious laws. There was no more land along the coast, but Fox said that behind New Jersey lay unoccupied fertile land with a great river leading up to it.

New Jersey had been divided between Lords Berkeley and Carteret; then some Quakers had bought Lord Berkeley's share. There was disagreement among them, and lawyer Penn was called in to arbitrate. Later he became a trustee of this West Jersey colony and helped draw up its "Concessions and Agreements." In this constitution of a sort, religious liberty was guaranteed, and freedom to vote, trial by jury, and an assembly elected by the people. Working on it was the best possible preparation Penn could have had for what lay ahead. For at last Penn became discouraged over the prospect of religious toleration in England, and out of that discouragement grew the dream of the "holy experiment" of Pennsylvania.

Admiral Penn had been one of many who had loaned extravagant Charles II money which had not been repaid. Now William Penn reasoned that by deeding to him, the admiral's heir, land in the New World, the King could at the same time satisfy his debt and rid himself of thousands of unwanted, troublesome Quakers. Penn formally petitioned Charles II for the land "bounded on the east by the Delaware River, on the west limited as Maryland, and northward to extend as far as plantable."

The King's Privy Council discussed the matter. It reviewed the neighboring colonies' boundaries and approved the King's deeding to William Penn a tract of land almost as large as England. The King named the huge area Pennsylvania, in honor of Admiral Penn. The admiral's son was to be its absolute proprietor, subject only to the King, for a fee of two beaverskins "to be delivered at our castle of Windsor on the first day of January in every year," and a fifth of any gold or silver found. The charter, like Lord Baltimore's fifty years earlier, guaranteed the colonists government through an assembly, but left Penn free to appoint magistrates and other officials.

William Penn at once began a vigorous campaign to get "adventurers" of every faith to settle the new colony. They could either rent or buy on very reasonable terms, and they could be sure of justice and religious freedom. "We must give the liberty we ask," Penn declared again and again. No one was to be "molested or prejudiced for their religious persuasion, or practice, in matters of faith and worship, nor shall they be compelled at any time to frequent or maintain any religious worship, place, or ministry whatsoever." Only atheists and criminals could not vote, and only non-Christians could not hold office.

Penn received help from many expert sources in preparing the Pennsylvania Frame of Government, and it went through no less than twenty drafts before reaching its final form. This became a model for many of the state Constitutions and for parts of the United States Constitution. It even provided for the future by specifying that the assembly could change it as the need arose.

Penn chose his cousin, William Markham, to serve as the first Governor of Pennsylvania. He gave him detailed instructions on many matters, including the laying out of Philadelphia, "City of Brotherly Love." Markham also carried a letter from Penn to the Indian chiefs of the region, assuring them that "the people who come are a just, plain, and honest people that neither make war upon others, nor fear war from others, because they will be just." Although Penn hoped to build a prosperous colony, he refused a trading company's offer for exclusive rights to the Indian trade for fear the company might treat the natives unfairly.

A year later, in 1682, Penn himself made the crossing. After being welcomed by Markham, the early settlers, and many Indians, he began an incredibly busy winter. He traveled great distances to inspect his province. He held meetings and started ambitious projects. He visited dozens of Indian chiefs to buy land from them and make treaties of friendship. Like Roger Williams, he learned their language and was accepted by them as a friend and councilor.

The Maryland boundary proved to be a troublesome matter. Because of hazy notions about the geography of the New World, Lord Baltimore's territory and that of William Penn overlapped by many miles. Repeated meetings between Penn and the third Lord Baltimore brought no agreement. Neither did Penn's letters to friends at court, nor even his sending Markham to England to present Pennsylvania's case in person. When armed Maryland men tried to collect taxes from Pennsylvania settlers, Penn hurried to see Lord Baltimore but found that he had left for England. Then Penn knew that he too must go.

While waiting for a hearing on the boundary dispute, Penn tried to help the Quakers, who were in a worse state than ever that fall of 1684. He managed to get many of them out of prison, but he could do little more. His hopes rose after the death of Charles II that winter, for he and the new King, James II, the former Duke of York, had long been friends. James was an ardent Catholic, who leaned heavily on the advice of his Catholic councilors, but he was also a naturally tolerant man. He regarded Penn as a close friend and wanted him at court. Penn returned the King's affection and trusted his promises of increased religious toleration. Many Quakers, however, resented Penn's spending so much time with the King and some of them believed the persistent rumors that William Penn was secretly a Catholic.

At last there was a partial settlement of the Maryland border dispute. Penn did not sail for Pennsylvania immediately because he was short of money and also because he felt duty bound to use his royal friendship to improve religious conditions in England. Then James's queen bore him a son, and the Protestants, foreseeing a Catholic England, deposed James and invited his son-in-law, Protestant William of Orange, to come with his wife Mary to rule over England. James put up only a feeble resistance and soon fled to France.

Penn, the acknowledged friend of James, was now in a bad position indeed. His Irish estates were confiscated, and he was questioned by the Privy Council three times. He even spent a short time in the Tower, but his straightforward explanation soon convinced the authorities that he was completely devoted to his country, even though he never denied his friendship for the former King. Ironically, the Quakers received from William and Mary the religious toleration which Penn had thought he could win from James II.

Things were going badly in Pennsylvania. Penn had given authority to the wrong people, and his agent was sending false accounts which Penn, with his characteristic blind trust of friends, continued to sign. He wrote long letters in a desperate effort to end quarrels, suppress feuds, and right wrongs in the colony.

When Penn was accused of disloyalty for the fourth time, and this time was charged with conspiring to reseat James on the English throne, he saw no virtue in going to the Tower and perhaps to his death on false charges. Instead, he went into hiding in or near London. Never idle, he used this three-year period to write a book of maxims and a treatise on achieving peace among the nations of Europe. In 1693, he was cleared of all charges. Pennsylvania, which had been taken from him, was returned, and he was allowed to move about and preach freely.

Principally because of financial difficulties, Penn did not return to Pennsylvania until six years later. This time he took with him a second wife, his young-lady daughter, and a capable and devoted secretary, James Logan. Penn hardly knew Philadelphia, for in the fifteen years since he had left it had grown to be the largest city, next to Boston, in the colonies. Settlers, new and old, and Indians of many tribes greeted him warmly. He was delighted to be back. He set to work to administer the affairs of the growing colony with his usual energy, enthusiasm, and ability. He made new peace treaties with Indian chiefs, revised the Pennsylvania Frame of Government, and even planned a conference of colonial Governors. Then news arrived that all proprietary colonies were to be put under the direct control of the Crown, and he must return to England.

Penn's personal affairs were in a great tangle. His dishonest agents had gained such power that they threw Penn into debtors' prison. No one in the colony seemed interested in helping him, so English Friends raised money to make a settlement and release him. His oldest son had died, and his next son had turned into a dissipated rake. A discouraged Penn wrote, "I cannot but think it hard measure that, while that [Pennsylvania] has proved a land of freedom and flourishing, it should become to me, by whose means it was principally made a country, the cause of grief, trouble, and poverty."

When Anne became Queen in 1702, Penn was again welcome at court. He started negotiations with the Crown for the sale of his New World rights, with the provision that Pennsylvania remain "a free colony for all mankind." He insisted that religious freedom be maintained, that Quakers not be forced to take oaths or to go into military service against their will, and that the Pennsylvania policy of peace based on justice be continued.

Agreement was nearly reached on all points when Penn suffered a stroke and his wife took over his affairs. She was able to keep the governorship of Pennsylvania for the younger members of the Penn family — a privilege which they held until the Revolution.

After a few feeble years, William Penn died. He was acknowledged by all to have been a great man. He had made a dream into reality, and had put into action his ideals of individual dignity, human brotherhood, and religious freedom. He would never be forgotten.

The care of every man's soul belongs to himself.

THOMAS JEFFERSON

All men are equally entitled to the free exercise of religion according to the dictates of conscience.

JAMES MADISON

Two Gentlemen of Virginia

Thomas Jefferson (1743–1826)
James Madison (1751–1836)

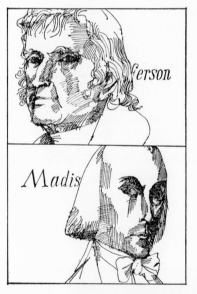

THOMAS JEFFERSON wanted to be remembered for three things: "Author of the Declaration of American Independence, of the Statute of Virginia for Religious Freedom, and Father of the University of Virginia." These were the words he directed to be carved on his tombstone—"and not a word more." Not even President of the United States.

Today Jefferson is best remembered for writing the Declaration of Independence, and his friend James Madison as

"Father of the Constitution." Yet it should also be remembered that these two men, more than any others, were responsible for freedom of religion in the new nation.

Thomas Jefferson's father passed on to his eldest son Tom much of the land he had acquired in the foothills of western Virginia and the family home, Shadwell. He also gave him a love for growing things and open spaces, a lively curiosity, and a keen sense of fair play. From his mother, a Randolph from the rich tidewater section of Virginia, Tom absorbed the traditions and manners of the aristocracy.

At seventeen, three years after his father's death, young Jefferson entered William and Mary College in Williamsburg. On the frontier he had learned some Latin and Greek, French, logic, and mathematics from clergymen teachers. At college he added to that knowledge. He also joined gaily in the social life of the little provincial capital. Because he played the violin, he was invited to the Governor's mansion to dine and play quartets with the British Governor, a Scottish professor, and a local lawyer. The lawyer, George Wythe, remained his friend for life.

Like many other young men of property and position, Jefferson took up the study of law after his graduation from college. As was the custom, he "read law" under a practicing lawyer — his friend Wythe. Much of his reading Jefferson did at Shadwell, where at the same time he could look after his lands and lead the free, outdoor life he enjoyed. A fine horseman, he found the journey to Williamsburg an easy one when he wanted to consult lawyer Wythe, buy or borrow law books, or visit friends.

While in college, Jefferson had become acquainted with Patrick Henry. Though without wealth or social standing, careless of his personal appearance, and with only slight legal training, Henry was a man to reckon with — a brilliant lawyer, afire with his belief in the rights of man and so eloquent that he could all but charm the birds off the branches. Henry, a member of the Virginia Assembly, was chosen to present its side in a case known as the "Parson's Cause."

For years the salaries of the Virginia clergymen of the established church, the Church of England, had been based on the current value of the colony's chief crop, tobacco. When the Assembly voted to base payment on a fixed tobacco price of twopence a pound, which was less than the usual rate, the clergymen objected. They appealed to the King's Privy Council in London, which reversed the Assembly's "Twopenny Act." A clergyman, who happened to be one of Jefferson's frontier teachers, sued for back pay based on the current, higher tobacco price. The jury in the case was to decide just how much he and the other clergymen were entitled to receive.

Jefferson listened eagerly as Henry argued that the King's Privy Council had no right to set aside a law legally passed by the Virginia Assembly. This, Henry claimed, was a tyrannical action which undermined the authority of the colonial body. The jurors were so impressed by Henry's arguments and his eloquence that they awarded the clergymen back pay of just one penny. Jefferson, too, was impressed. What, he wondered, had been the relationship between government and religion in past times? Did a Government have the right to set up an official religion and tax people for its support? Should the Virginia "dissenters" — those people who had turned away from the established, official Church of England — be taxed to pay the salaries of its clergymen?

Jefferson dug into old English law, but could find no historic legal grounds for a King or Government to dictate the religious belief of its people. After reading English and French philosophers, talking to Henry and Wythe and others, and doing much solitary thinking on the subject, Jefferson came to the conclusion that freedom of worship was a natural right and that churches should be entirely separate from the state, with no one sect dominating the others. It was not a popular belief among most of his friends.

Patrick Henry's bold challenging of the authority of the Privy Council over the Virginia Assembly also jolted Jefferson. So did the fiery lawyer's defiance of the British Parliament when it imposed a stamp tax on the colonies. Jefferson was a loyal subject of the motherland, but he saw no reason why British subjects living in America should not have exactly the same rights as British subjects living in England. He was relieved when Parliament repealed the hated Stamp Act.

After finishing his law studies, Jefferson was admitted to the bar and began to practice law. From the start he had plenty of cases. His knowledge of law, his logical mind, and his habit of thorough research were in his favor, but he was no orator like his friend Henry. For several years, however, Jefferson made a good income as a lawyer. Then, because of his growing interest in government and in scientific farming, he left the law, though all his life he found his knowledge of it useful.

Albemarle County elected Jefferson to represent its

people in the 1769 Virginia Assembly. Jefferson rode to Williamsburg and took his place as a burgess. Five days later the British Governor dissolved the Assembly for daring to pass resolutions objecting to taxation without representation in Parliament and recommending closer cooperation among the colonies. Young Jefferson was one of the eighty-eight burgesses who met the next day in the Raleigh Tavern to form an independent association. Before they adjourned they pledged themselves not to buy certain articles imported from England, as George Mason recommended in his "Resolves," which George Washington presented. As the burgesses rode to their homes they wondered anxiously what lay ahead.

Ever since he was a boy, Jefferson had dreamed of having a home at the top of a small mountain near Shadwell. Its long view appealed to him so strongly that he refused to be daunted by the tremendous task of creating an estate on a mountaintop. Building Monticello (Little Mountain) was a labor of love which went on over many years, with Jefferson himself the architect, contractor, and overseer. He planned it for gracious yet convenient living, and it became one of the showplaces of America. Luckily one section was completed in 1770, for that year Shadwell burned to the ground, destroying all of Jefferson's treasured books and papers. He moved up the mountain and kept bachelor hall at Monticello. Two years later, when it was nearer completion, he brought to it his bride, a lovely and accomplished young widow.

All too soon Jefferson had to give up the enjoyable life of a scholarly country gentleman. As the colonies' troubles with Great Britain multiplied, he found himself in the thick of everything. Because of his facility in writing, he was put on the Correspondence Committee, which was responsible for providing closer contact with the other colonies. When the British closed Boston port in retaliation for the Boston Tea Party, Jefferson helped arrange for a day of fasting and prayer in protest. All over the colony men and women filled the churches to hear clergymen pray that God would "turn the hearts of the King and Parliament to moderation and justice."

On his way to the 1774 Williamsburg Convention — the independent successor to the Virginia Assembly — Jefferson was taken ill and had to return home. He sent on his written suggestions for instructions to the delegates to be sent to the first Continental Congress to meet in Philadelphia in September. The Convention thought Jefferson's ideas too bold to follow, but agreed that his presentation of colonial grievances was so clear and forceful that it should be printed. The pamphlet, called *A Summary View of the Rights of British America,* was reprinted in Philadelphia and in London, and opened many eyes to the difficulties in the relationship between the King and his American colonies.

At the second Virginia Convention, held in Richmond in 1775, Jefferson heard Patrick Henry make his stirring speech urging the colony to arm for defense. The same Convention appointed Jefferson a delegate to the Continental Congress. Arriving in Philadelphia after ten days' driving, he was immediately put on a committee with Benjamin Franklin, John Adams, and Richard Lee, to answer the "Conciliatory Proposals" of Lord North. It was Jefferson who was responsible for the "well-reasoned," respectful, but firm rejection adopted by Congress.

Most of that winter Jefferson spent at home because of

the failing health of his wife and of his mother. While at Monticello he organized the Albemarle County militia and wrote many letters regarding the colonial situation. By May, when he returned to Philadelphia, he was convinced that the colonies must become independent. Like so many others he had been deeply impressed by Thomas Paine's *Common Sense,* which held that the colonies should no longer endure the oppressive acts of King and Parliament. He was glad that the Virginia Convention had instructed its delegates to the Congress to propose that it issue a formal declaration of the colonies' independence.

In order to prepare themselves for self-government, the Congress recommended that each colony draft a Constitution for itself. Jefferson spent long evenings planning one for Virginia, changing old British procedures to fit New World conditions. He sent his "Proposed Constitution for Virginia" to the Virginia Convention by messenger, but it arrived too late to be used, except for a few paragraphs in the preamble. Much of it probably would have been rejected anyway, for it called for "complete toleration of religious opinions," a free press, and the abolition of slavery.

In Philadelphia, Jefferson was one of a committee of five appointed to draft a Declaration of Independence, and the one chosen to write it. He wrote at white heat, drawing on his vast reading and study, his legal knowledge, his intense convictions, and on Mason's work for the Virginia Declaration. His draft was approved with only minor changes — and the omission of the section on slavery — and on July fourth, 1776, the bell rang out to announce the momentous decision for independence.

After helping draw up the Articles of Confederation to bind the colonies into a single Government, Jefferson returned to the Virginia Convention. It was here that he and Madison became close friends.

Like Jefferson, Madison had grown up on a Virginia plantation within sight of the Blue Ridge Mountains. As a boy and as a man he, too, loved the out-of-doors yet eagerly sought the knowledge to be found in books. Both boys were taught by Scottish clergymen schoolmasters, then went off to college — Jefferson to Virginia's William and Mary, and Madison to Princeton, then the College of New Jersey. This choice was made partly because the climate of the Northern college town was better than that of low-lying Williamsburg, and young Madison was somewhat undersized and delicate.

At college Madison studied theology and law although, like Jefferson, he had a poor voice for public speaking. Excited by the revolutionary spirit which was strong on the campus, he became active in the college's newly formed American Whig Society. Already he believed strongly in religious liberty and was quick to argue in favor of freedom of conscience and against a tax-supported established church.

After graduating at twenty, Madison stayed on at Princeton for several months to study ethics, Hebrew, and the "principles and modes of government." Then he returned to Montpelier, the family home in Virginia's Orange County, where he went on with his reading and study and tutored his younger brothers and sisters.

Madison was angry when several clergymen in the next

county were jailed because of their religious opinions. In writing a Philadelphia friend he lamented that religious liberty, "which is one of the characteristics of a free people," was not observed in Virginia as in Pennsylvania. "I have squabbled and scolded, abused and ridiculed so long about it to little purpose that I am without common patience," he wrote. "So I must beg you to pity me and pray for liberty of conscience for all."

In 1774, Madison visited his friend in Philadelphia and went on to New York, but was home soon after the British Governor for the second time dissolved the Virginia Assembly. With his father he helped raise men and supplies for the Orange County militia, and through a wide correspondence he kept the local Committee of Public Safety informed on the activities of the British in various parts of the country and of the Congress in Philadelphia.

In the spring of 1776, Orange County elected twenty-five-year-old Madison to the Virginia Convention, meeting again in Williamsburg. It was, he said, "my first entrance into public life." The colonial capital was alive with men in uniform and mountaineers with long rifles. Off the coast lay hostile warships commanded by Virginia's former royal Governor. Members of the Convention knew very well that if their great move for independence failed, they faced probable death.

Madison helped count the votes which made Patrick Henry Virginia's first American Governor, and was on George Mason's committee to draw up a Declaration of Rights and a state Constitution. He begged leave to differ with one Article in Mr. Mason's Bill of Rights — the one having to do with religion. Did not the word *toleration* in the phrase "All men should enjoy the fullest toleration in the exercise of religion" imply that any disagreement was by the gracious consent of those in authority? Yet was it not "the inborn right of every man to worship as he chose without the need of any other man's consent"? Mr. Mason looked thoughtfully at the soft-spoken, earnest young delegate from Orange County, then invited him to reword the Article.

Madison's first draft recommended that the state abolish its established church, but as this was disapproved by most of the committee it did not appear in the next draft. Madison's final version, which was approved by the committee and adopted without debate by the Convention, set the dictates of conscience above the authority of the state for the first time anywhere. "The religion, or the duty which we owe to our Creator," it stated, "and the manner of discharging it, can be directed only by reason and conviction, not by force or violence; and therefore all men are equally entitled to the free exercise of religion according to the dictates of conscience." This statement was hailed as "a rising sun of religious liberty," and was followed by other states and by the young nation.

With both the Bill of Rights and the state Constitution worked out, the Convention adjourned, unaware that the colonies' Declaration of Independence from England was about to be signed in Philadelphia.

All delegates to the Virginia Convention were automatically members of the new state Assembly which met that fall of 1776. Madison was delighted that Jefferson was there, and very soon the two men discovered how much they had in common. Both worked to replace the antiquated Virginia laws with more liberal ones. Jefferson introduced more than a hundred bills, most of which were made into law, thanks to the help of Madison, Mason, and Wythe. One change was to allow all the children of a family to inherit an estate instead of just the eldest son, as in England; this broke the grip of Virginia's landed aristocracy. Another was to legalize marriages made outside the established church. One of Jefferson's bills which did not pass would have provided for free district grammar schools and a free state college and library; another would have abolished slavery.

But the bill which stirred up the biggest hornets' nest was Jefferson's Bill for Establishing Religious Freedom. Mason's Bill of Rights, while specifying religious freedom, did not disturb the status of the established church. Presbyterians and Baptists in Virginia, who outnumbered two to one members of the Church of England, now called the Episcopal Church, wanted to outlaw the state-supported church. They agreed with Jefferson's Bill which stated, "Almighty God hath created the mind free," and declared in Section I, "To compel a man to furnish contributions of money for the propagation of opinions which he disbelieves and abhors, is sinful and tyrannical . . . The opinions of men are not the object of civil government, nor under its jurisdiction." Section II went on, "We the General Assembly of Virginia do enact that no man shall be compelled to frequent or support any religious worship, place, or ministry, nor shall he be enforced, restrained, molested, or burthened in his body or goods, or shall otherwise suffer, on account of his religious opinions or belief; but that all men shall be free . . .

argument to maintain, their opinions in matters of religion, and that the same shall in no wise diminish, enlarge, or affect their civil capacities."

But Virginia legislators, most of whom belonged to the state church, were not yet ready to go to such lengths. They did, however, repeal laws requiring dissenters to contribute to the established church and laws which punished them for staying away from services. This halfway action did not satisfy either Jefferson or Madison. "The care of every man's soul belongs to himself," Jefferson insisted, and Madison agreed.

To Madison's disappointment, he was not elected to the next legislative session. He had balked at following the old British custom of gaining votes by treating his constituency to free whiskey, and a less scrupulous man had won the seat. But Madison was not out of public service for long. The following year the Assembly made him a member of an advisory Council of State to Governor Henry, with the special duty of managing details connected with the war. In spite of British armies coming closer and closer to Virginia, Madison approved the Governor's decision to send food and clothing to George Washington's starving, threadbare army in the North. By the time Jefferson succeeded Henry as Governor in 1779, Virginia had sent Washington so much money and equipment and so many men that there was little left for its own defense. Jefferson worked desperately, with the help of Madison and others, to solve Virginia's financial and military problems, but the enemy overran the state, and Jefferson was blamed for it. Before Jefferson's unhappy two-year term was over, Madison had left the Council to become a Virginia delegate to the Continental Congress. He was thrilled at this chance to play a part in national affairs, but appalled at the serious problems the new nation faced. Continental money was losing all value, the British were capturing city after city, and every state seemed to think only of itself.

Madison put his disciplined brain and vast store of knowledge to work. As each matter came up he calmly, relentlessly pursued it to its logical conclusion and then presented his facts to the Congress. Despite his shyness, his small stature, and his weak voice, he spoke impressively, and the delegates listened.

The nation's problems did not end with Cornwallis's surrender at Yorktown. There was the peace treaty to be negotiated, the soldiers to be paid — from an empty treasury — and the independent, quarreling states somehow to be welded into a smoothly working union. It was Madison who helped persuade them to stop issuing worthless paper money and to cede their Western lands to the nation so that the soldiers might be paid in land grants. But since no delegate was permitted to succeed himself, Madison went back to Virginia at the end of his term in 1783.

That same year Jefferson returned to the Congress, after a sorrowful interval at Monticello. During the long months of his wife's last illness he wrote his only book, the informative *Notes on Virginia*. Then again he played his large part in shaping and strengthening the new nation. With Robert Morris he worked out its currency system and, practically alone, planned the government of the Western lands turned over by the states. His proposal to abolish slavery in them, which would have prevented the War between the States, lost by just one vote. At the request of Congress he journeyed to Paris to help Benjamin Franklin and John Adams make trade treaties with European countries, then stayed on to succeed the aging Franklin as minister to France.

Madison, after spending a year at home studying law, was again elected to the Virginia Assembly's House of Delegates, now meeting in Richmond. As a member of the Committee on Religion he opposed a bill introduced by Patrick Henry for the support of teachers of the Christian religion. Many people could not understand why religious teachers should not be paid by public taxation, like other teachers, but Madison's keen mind saw that making payments to religious sects from the public treasury for purposes of religious instruction would lead to state control of other religious matters. By making an effective speech he succeeded in having the final vote postponed until the next session. Before then, he wrote out his arguments and had the pamphlet *Memorial and Remonstrance against Religious Assessments* printed and distributed all over the state. So many people read and signed the *Remonstrance* that Henry's bill was soundly defeated.

Then Madison reintroduced Jefferson's Bill for Establishing Religious Freedom. With Jefferson serving the nation in France, it had lain over from session to session. Now Madison maneuvered, persuaded, and fought for it. Episcopal clergymen and many others still wanted to keep the state church. But the number of dissenters in Virginia had grown, and in 1780, Madison was able to get Jefferson's Bill made into law. This "Magna Carta of religious liberty," which made all religious faiths equal before the law, marked the real beginning of the separation of church and state. In Europe, where the Act was translated into French and Italian, Jefferson watched its influence spread. Before many years this American-born idea became almost universally accepted.

Madison was a delegate to the Convention convened in 1787 to consider the young nation's foreign and domestic problems. After long hours of study he decided that the Articles of Confederation were too weak and full of flaws to be revised; that the nation needed an entirely new constitution. With the other delegates from his state he worked out the Virginia Plan, which became the keystone of the Convention discussions.

During the long hot summer, fifty-five devoted men from thirteen vastly different states hammered out a new form of government. Nearly always it was Madison who contributed most to the lengthy debates, who suggested possible compromises or necessary revisions, who persuaded individual states to give up powers to the central Government. When, in September, the work was finally done, it must have seemed like a miracle to every man there. The Constitution of the United States of America was, in truth, Madison's concept of "a federal republic ruled by the people, with checks and balances to guard against tyranny." Modestly he insisted it was "the work of many heads and many hands," but no one questioned that the title "Father of the Constitution" rightfully belonged to James Madison.

Yet there were complaints, and the one oftenest heard was that the Constitution lacked guarantees of freedom of religion, of speech and press, and of trial by jury. It hurt Madison that he was accused of having "ceased to be a friend to the rights of conscience" because he had not recommended including a Bill of Rights in the Constitution.

In the famous *Federalist* papers he pointed out that to specify certain rights might seem to exclude others. Yet the all-important thing, Madison saw, was to put the Constitution into force as quickly as possible. And so, since some states threatened not to ratify the Constitution without a Bill of Rights, Mason agreed to try to get Congress to add such a Bill to the Constitution. On this promise he won Virginia's ratification.

True to his word, Madison proposed the Bill of Rights in the first session of Congress. Many of its Articles were suggested by George Mason and by leaders in other states. After debate, the Bill of Rights was added to the Constitution as its first ten Amendments, and before the close of 1791, enough states had ratified them to make them into law.

Madison took great pains with the wording of the clause relating to religion. He proposed that Congress should guarantee that "the civil rights of none should be abridged on account of religious belief or worship, nor shall any national religion be established, nor shall the full and equal rights of conscience be in any manner or on any pretext abridged." After several rewordings, this clause finally ended as the beginning to the familiar First Amendment: "Congress shall make no law respecting an establishment of religion, or prohibiting the free exercise thereof."

For forty-three years James Madison had remained a bachelor. Now, a leader in Congress and a valued adviser to President Washington, he married vivacious Dolly Todd, whose name became almost as well known as her husband's.

Jefferson never remarried. On his return after five years

as American minister to France, he was invited by President Washington to become the first Secretary of State. He agreed, although he would have preferred either to stay at Monticello or to return to Paris. He had a hard time in the Cabinet because many of his views were in direct conflict with those of another Cabinet member, Alexander Hamilton. After constant political strife for one term and part of the next, the President finally accepted Jefferson's resignation.

The country would not permit Jefferson to remain long at Monticello. In the presidential election following Washington's retirement, John Adams received the greatest number of votes and Jefferson the next greatest number. According to the then current procedure, that meant that Jefferson became Vice President under Adams — a difficult arrangement, since Adams was a conservative and Jefferson a liberal. Hamilton, infuriated by Jefferson's influence over President Adams, spread all sorts of misstatements to discredit him. He called him "an atheist in religion and a fanatic in politics," and many believed these false accusations. They did not understand Jefferson's refusal to discuss his own beliefs, or his sincere respect for others' religious opinions, no matter what they were. Many, too, still held against him his fight to abolish an established church and to separate church and state completely.

The 1800 presidential campaign was a bitter one. Ministers of the Congregational Church, which was still the established church in New England, feared the loss of their power if Jefferson were elected, and spread ugly rumors about him. Jefferson answered them only by stating firmly, "I am for freedom of religion and against all maneuvers to bring about a legal ascendancy of one sect over another." And he declared, "I have sworn upon the altar of God eternal hostility against every form of tyranny over the mind of man."

The mud spattered by pulpit and press did not prevent Jefferson's election, though it was a close thing. But Jefferson's inaugural address put many fears to rest by its moderate tone and its dedication to the finest principles of democracy.

It surprised no one that Jefferson made Madison, who had been serving in the Virginia legislature during part of Adams's administration, his Secretary of State. The two men thought alike on almost everything, and Madison's analytical mind and keen political sense complemented Jefferson's remarkable talents and compelling personality.

For eight years, while Madison served in Jefferson's Cabinet, where he was easily the most influential member, his wife Dolly played official hostess in the White House for the widowed President. Like Jefferson, Madison saw the importance of trade on the Mississippi and heartily approved the Louisiana Purchase and the Lewis and Clark exploration of the West. But he disagreed with Jefferson's placing an embargo on American shipping in an effort to prevent war with either England or France.

When, on Jefferson's retirement after two terms, Madison was overwhelmingly elected President, he immediately withdrew the embargo. Foreign problems, however, continued to plague him, and at last Henry Clay's strong war party pushed him into a senseless war with England. Peace came just in time to save the Government from collapse and its President from disgrace. With his talent for peacetime leadership, Madison built up the nation, so that before the end of his second term the Republic was prospering, and he and Dolly were again popular with the people.

Madison's deep interest in religious freedom led him as President to veto several bills which he said exceeded the rightful authority of the Government in "the essential distinction between civil and religious functions." In many letters he wrote in his later life he insisted on the "perfect equality of rights in the United States for every religious sect" and stated, "There is not a shadow of right in the general Government to intermeddle with religion."

After the presidency Madison, like Jefferson, retired to his Virginia home. At Montpelier he applied himself to practical farming matters, received many visitors, kept up his interest in politics, and wrote numerous letters and articles. Like Jefferson, he disapproved of the institution of slavery, yet kept slaves.

Jefferson's delight in gracious living and abundant hospitality and in continually adding to Monticello's beauty or convenience — often through his own imaginative mechanical inventions — badly depleted his purse. When Monticello was threatened, the "unsolicited offerings of love" sent by several Northern cities saved it from forced sale. The major interest of Jefferson's last years was the creation of the University of Virginia in nearby Charlottesville. He was its founder, planner, architect, and manager. Madison, who also regarded education as the cornerstone of an intelligent citizenry, worked with him in establishing the university and in selecting its faculty. And after Jefferson's death on July 4, 1826, Madison succeeded him as its rector.

To the end, Jefferson's mind was active and questing, and his broad vision altogether in keeping with the motto he had chosen for the University of Virginia: "Ye shall know the truth and the truth shall make you free."

The "great little Madison" grew old peacefully, though crippled with rheumatism. After his death at eighty-five, a paper was found which he had headed "Advice to My Country," and on which he had written, "The advice nearest to my heart and deepest in my conviction is THAT THE UNION OF THE STATES BE CHERISHED AND PERPETUATED."

The cause of religious liberty was equally dear to James Madison and to Thomas Jefferson. Their devoted, persistent championship of it, against heavy odds, was largely responsible for the freedom of religious belief and worship treasured in the United States of America.

Diversity with Understanding

The National Conference of Christians and Jews (founded 1928)

WHEN the Bill of Rights became national law, back in 1791, some people believed—and more of them hoped—that now every American citizen could truly worship as he chose. But it was one thing for the Government to pledge this and another for the people to cooperate. To be sure, there was no longer the violence of early colonial days, when colonists of one faith actually fought those of other faiths. For the most part, open discrimination against Catholics, Jews,

Quakers, and other religious minorities disappeared after the Revolution. Anyone could now hold office, whatever his religion. But there was still a big gap between the attitude of most Americans and that of such men as Jefferson and Madison.

Most of those who thought about the matter were vaguely proud that their country had given the world this great new concept of religious freedom. Every one of the states that came into the Union after the original thirteen guaranteed full religious liberty in its Constitution. (Two of the thirteen, though, held out against it for a long time. Connecticut kept its royal charter with its established church — Congregational — and its controlling Standing Order — the ministry — until 1818, when its new Constitution guaranteed religious freedom to everyone "without discrimination." And it was 1833 before Massachusetts added a religious-liberty amendment to its Constitution.)

Americans learned slowly that Old World prejudices did not fit well in American life, and that men and women of many different faiths actually could live together harmoniously, as useful citizens of a democratic country.

But prejudice is hard to forget and easy to rouse. In the 1830's, an influx of Irish Catholics worried the old Protestant settlers into joining together in a sort of America-for-Americans movement. These "nativists" attacked Catholics in many unfair, illegal ways, and sometimes even with violence. Times were hard, and this played a large part in the religious fanaticism. Many native Americans, seeing immigrants competing for their jobs, quickly forgot their belief in religious freedom and their good intentions of getting along with people of different convictions and backgrounds.

The anti-Catholic feeling died down as the economic situation improved, but it flared up again in the 1850's when the potato famine in Ireland drove a second wave of Irish Catholics to America. They were tolerated as cheap laborers, but not many treated them as human beings with human rights. The members of a secret organization, the Know-Nothing party, pledged themselves to fight the Catholic Church and immigration. For a few years the Know-Nothings had real power, then the movement faded away as slavery became the nation's number-one issue. Not until the 1890's was another powerful secret "hate" society formed. This was the American Protective Association, set up to fight Catholicism and the second-generation immigrants, who were fast becoming economic rivals.

The Jewish minority had, on the whole, fewer troubles in nineteenth-century America than the Catholic. In Maryland, a Presbyterian named Kennedy won for the Jews full religious freedom in that state. Even though the nativists' intolerance did not touch them much, the Jews worked against it in an effort to safeguard religious liberty for all. But when more Jewish immigrants arrived, first from Germany and then from Russia, the Jews, too, felt the sting of discrimination.

The worst hate movement in the country's history came in the restless nationalistic period following World War I. Then the Ku Klux Klan, which had been formed fifty years before to intimidate Negroes and carpetbaggers in the South, was revived. Its aim of "native, white, Protestant supremacy" was dramatized by fiery burning crosses, night-riding white-hooded figures, terrifying threats, public flog-gings and private murders. Widely circulated false state-ments about Catholics and Jews whipped up feeling until more than four million misguided persons joined the KKK. Henry Ford added to the tension by sponsoring a publica-tion filled with untruths about the Jews. It took a nation-wide newspaper campaign and a congressional investiga-tion to put an end to most of the KKK activities. After a time Mr. Ford, realizing that he had been misinformed, made a public apology and started trying to promote brotherhood instead of hatred.

Another batch of venom was let loose in 1928, when for the first time a Catholic ran for the presidency. The strong statement of Governor Alfred Smith, the candidate, opened many eyes to the unfairness of the propaganda being whis-pered around. After professing his belief in absolute free-dom of conscience for all, in the brotherhood of man under the fatherhood of God, and in the strict enforcement of the First Amendment, Governor Smith expressed the hope that "never again in this land will any public servant be chal-lenged because of the faith in which he has tried to walk humbly with his God."

It required more than individual effort to combat out-breaks of religious bigotry like these. Teamwork definitely was needed. And so, that year of 1928, leaders of the various faiths organized the National Conference of Chris-tians and Jews. Its first officials were former Secretary of War Newton D. Baker, a Protestant; Professor Carlton Hayes, a Catholic; and Roger Straus, a Jew. Their aim was to develop mutual understanding among people of different faiths — "the only secure foundation for an abiding de-

mocracy." They hoped "to moderate — and finally to eliminate — a system of prejudices which disfigures and distorts
our business, social, and political relations," and to establish "a basis of cooperation for common ends while insuring
the rights of individuals and groups to differ." For, as
Charles Evans Hughes, an active leader in the interfaith
movement and soon to become Chief Justice, warned,
"When we lose the right to be different, we lose the right to
be free."

The National Conference of Christians and Jews undertook a long-range, nationwide program of intergroup
education. Since it was a civic organization and did not officially represent any religious bodies, it could explain various viewpoints objectively. It could also emphasize common aims and point the way to understanding, respect, and
cooperation.

The "trio team" was an early, dramatic form of the
organization's educational program. A panel consisting of a
priest, a minister, and a rabbi went from city to city to
present and discuss their different viewpoints and their
much wider areas of agreement. The visible friendship
among the three men struck a blow against intolerance even
before a word was spoken. Their frank answers to questions
promoted a healthy respect for too-little-understood faiths,
and their helpful suggestions sparked many worthwhile
intergroup activities.

Discussion groups, made up of citizens belonging to
different faiths, were organized by the National Conference
of Christians and Jews in many places. In these regularly
scheduled meetings candid conversations uncovered various
pressures, which discussion often minimized and sometimes

even solved. Round tables, seminars, and institutes were set up on college and university campuses to find ways of improving human relations. Camp conferences, parent-teacher workshops, and labor-management get-togethers aired tensions and opened the way for coordinated inter-faith projects. Underlying all these discussion groups was the principle that in a society where citizens agree to disagree in their religious beliefs, everyone has a responsi-bility to learn to live with those differences and to handle them so that they will contribute to the common good. The immature "I don't like you because you're different" can change to the more mature "Your difference makes you interesting; I want to know you better," and then become "Let's work together for a better community, for a better America."

In 1934, the National Conference of Christians and Jews sponsored its first Brotherhood Week. President Franklin Roosevelt endorsed it warmly, dedicating it "not to the things which divide but to the things which unite us." He urged all citizens to take part in this "venture in neighborli-ness," and reminded them that respecting honest differences of opinion was part of the American heritage. Since that year, Brotherhood Week has been an annual February affair, celebrated in thousands of American communities with banquets, programs, and various school and commu-nity intergroup activities. Its inspiring slogans, beginning with "Make America safe for differences," have gone on with "Brotherhood begins in the hearts of men," and "Brotherhood is YOUR business."

The anti-Jewish atrocities in Germany under Hitler shocked Americans deeply. The Nazi attempts to spread their doctrines in the United States did not get far. The NCCJ, as the interfaith organization came to be known, brought hate incidents into the open and showed them to be both despicable in themselves and inconsistent with American democracy.

The NCCJ set up a Religious News Service to provide several hundred newspapers with items of interest about different faiths in this and other countries and especially to feature incidents of happy interrelationships among various faiths. The Religious News Service also began providing year-round programs on TV and radio, to bring the concept of brotherhood closer home to every American. Much printed informational material has been prepared and distributed by the National Conference of Christians and Jews from its start. This ranges from learned papers for the scholarly, on such subjects as the changing meanings of religious freedom in America, problems of church and state, and religious responsibility for the social order, to simple leaflets for the general reader. In these, the purpose of the NCCJ is explained in simple language and ways are suggested for helping "bring mutual understanding into our national life."

A Ford Foundation grant to the organization in 1961 underwrote a National Council of Public Affairs and Religious Freedom. Its purpose was to analyze political difficulties created by conflicting religious approaches to social problems. In a National Institute experts discussed judicial and legislative decisions which affected religion. A Religious Press Institute talked about how a responsible church press should deal with controversial issues. "Dialogue Groups" of rabbis, priests, and ministers were organized in more than forty cities to meet regularly to discuss religious and public affairs. A "discussion film" was made to show the interreligious tensions in a small community over school transportation. Other films and publications are available for community study-action programs.

A NCCJ project termed "Rearing Children of Good Will" sponsors regional and national institutes for parents to emphasize the importance of teaching children attitudes suited to democratic living. Other institutes and conferences provide youth leaders with an opportunity to discuss issues of concern to them. A police-community relations project brings together police officials to discuss methods of dealing with minority groups. Still another project, addressed to business executives and labor leaders, studies "Labor, Management, and Public Interest."

Social progress in the United States brings with it many problems, not a few of which involve religious matters. The separation of church and state guaranteed in the Constitution is interpreted differently by people with different religious viewpoints. Should the "wall of separation" recommended by Jefferson be high or low? How can differences be worked out in a sensible, friendly manner?

In the first one hundred fifty-eight years after the passage of the First Amendment, the Supreme Court had only one case brought before it concerned with the constitutional guarantee of religious freedom. This case, which involved the Mormons' idea of plural marriages, was rejected as incompatible with the nation's accepted social standards. Since 1940, the Supreme Court has been flooded with cases seeking to test the religious-freedom guarantee. One involved expressing patriotism by saluting the flag. The Court ruled that when this is felt to be a violation of conscience, conscience comes first and that the act of saluting the flag is not essential to patriotism. In another case the Court held that distributing religious literature from door to door is permissible, since it does not interfere with public order or infringe on others' rights.

The matter of religion in the schools poses a puzzling problem. There is honest disagreement as to what place religion should have in the schools of a religiously diverse society. There is no simple formula. Reaching a just solution requires understanding the issues and being sensitive to a variety of opinions.

In our fast-changing world social problems involving religious issues may make some intergroup tension inevitable. But Americans who want to keep their country strong cannot afford the luxury of impulsive, immature emotional outbreaks, of intolerant thinking, or of unfair action.

The National Conference of Christians and Jews, as it pursues its "trail-blazing American adventure in brotherhood," will continue to help individuals and communities gain the understanding and achieve the maturity to accommodate to religious differences. With a spirit of good citizenship and goodwill, this should not be too difficult.

III

THE THIRD IS
FREEDOM FROM WANT

Our knowledge and our aspirations have brought within reach the capacity to create, in freedom, a world without want.

PAUL G. HOFFMAN

A WORLD *where everyone has enough to eat and to wear and a decent place to live was a fantastic dream almost up to this present generation. Poverty was taken for granted; it was no-body's responsibility. Children sang, "Rattle his bones over the stones; he's only a pauper whom nobody owns." Good-hearted people put a penny into the beggar's cup but did nothing about changing the conditions that might have made it necessary for the poor man to beg. The founding fathers who guaranteed freedom of speech and of religion did not think of guaranteeing freedom from want. Men were poor either from misfortune or from shiftlessness, and neither of these conditions was the concern of the state!*

Accepting national responsibility for poverty was an idea which grew slowly. A century ago no one had heard the term "social consciousness" or thought of widespread poverty as a blot on society and something basically wrong and unjust.

Here and there a few conscientious persons concerned themselves with improving housing and health and working conditions. But with the development of America's rich natural resources, with an expanding economy and a rapidly rising standard of living, many people began to regard poverty as both wicked and absurd. Yet Franklin Roosevelt, in 1941, was the first world leader to express the conviction that freedom from want was an obligation and a possibility.

Now that conviction is shared by multitudes. All over the world, as well as in our own country, men and women are working to hasten the day when every human being will be truly free from want and from the perpetual, haunting fear of the morrow.

The slum is a problem not only of government, but of humanity.

The Most Useful American

Jacob A. Riis *(1849–1914)*

I N THE OLD TOWN of Ribe, Denmark, a fifteen-year-old boy left school and became apprenticed to the local carpenter. It was a bitter blow to the boy's father, senior master in the Latin School, who wanted this third son of his to be a scholar. But Jacob disliked school and wanted to get ahead in a trade. After a few months with the local carpenter he went to the great city of Copenhagen, where he worked with a master builder for four years. Then, his apprenticeship over, he went back to Ribe. But since the girl he was in love with there turned him down, and there was not much opportunity for a master carpenter in the small town, Jacob Riis set off in June 1870 for America. He had his belongings in a small trunk and a little more than enough money to pay for his passage. Luckily he could read and speak English with ease, though naturally he spoke with a decided Danish accent.

In New York young Riis soon found that there was, as he put it, "no special public clamor for my services." He hired out with a gang of men going to an ironworks in the Alleghenies, where he built huts for miners. He disliked the mountainous country, so different from the flat meadows and rolling dunes of his homeland. When he heard of a war in Europe in which his small country was involved, he rushed back to New York in a burst of patriotism, bent on enlisting. This was harder to do than he had expected, and he met with one rebuff after another. Before long his possessions were gone and he was almost penniless. He would not beg, but he did sample the filthy overnight lodging rooms of the city police stations and hated them from then on. He headed out of the city and for months eked out a bare living in New Jersey and upstate New York by laying bricks, working on farms, logging, and trapping. Then he found he had a talent for salesmanship, and he roamed over much of New York and Pennsylvania, selling first tables, then flatirons. Deciding there was no future in this, he returned to the city of New York and spent the last of his few dollars on a course in telegraphy.

Riis liked to write. In one of New York's smaller cities he had applied for a reporter's job. The editor turned him down, sneering at his presumption. Riis walked away, eyes flashing. At that moment he determined that nothing would stop him from someday becoming a newspaper reporter, and a good one. He found what he hoped was an opportunity on Long Island, but it turned out to be no more than two weeks' hard work and no pay. To make a living, he peddled books from door to door. Quite by accident he met the principal of the telegraphy school he had attended, who told him about an opening on Newspaper Row for a bright young man. The beginning salary was ten dollars a week. Riis applied and got the job.

He worked at gathering news and writing it up with, he said, "a furious kind of energy." His working day stretched from ten in the morning until after midnight. Riis's industry and enthusiasm made up in part for his lack of experience, and he learned quickly. The second year he bettered his salary by moving to Brooklyn to work on a four-page local weekly run by politicians. When their need for the paper was over, Riis was able to buy it from them with a down payment of only seventy-five dollars. He managed to save enough to pay the balance within a few months by doing practically everything himself. He gathered the news, solicited the advertisements, carried the printed sheets from the printer's to his office, and found the newsboys to peddle them. One day, to his surprise and delight, he received an affectionate letter from the girl he loved in Denmark. He immediately sold the paper — at a good profit — and rushed back to Ribe to claim her as his bride and bring her to America.

After selling advertising for a while, Riis became a newspaper reporter on the *New York Tribune*. An assignment to the Mulberry Street police headquarters started him on his life work, though he did not know it at the time. His job was to get the "trouble" news before it reached the courts — or the other papers. To do this, he hung around the police station and health department and went in and out of the alleys, back streets, tenements, saloons, and factories of this, the city's worst neighborhood. Reporters from rival newspapers gave him a rough time. Occasionally, when they sent him on a wild-goose chase at midnight, he turned the tables on them by ferreting out something they had missed. Years later they agreed that Jake Riis, by his energy and ability, had really earned his title of "boss reporter" of Mulberry Street.

Jacob Riis really cared about his work. He had a talent for discovering what lay behind a piece of news and of writing it up so that the reader caught its human drama. Yet his reporting was not sensational; he was always careful to base his statements on solid facts, and he would go to any amount of trouble to uncover those facts. Once he went to great pains to track down seemingly isolated cases of trichinosis and succeeded in finding their common source — poisoned ham sandwiches. Another time he read in a health department report that there was a "trace of nitrites" in the city's drinking water and by inquiring learned that this indicated sewage contamination. Through his paper he warned the public to boil its drinking water, then left — with his camera — for the source of the New York City water supply. He spent a week at the Croton River and its tributaries gathering evidence. His illustrated story, at first pooh-poohed by other papers, led the Board of Health to dispatch inspectors to the city water source. Their report showed that the contamination was even worse than Riis had stated, and as a result the city took drastic measures to clean up the situation and so avert a possible epidemic.

The slum area Jacob Riis worked in made a deep impression on him. Every day he became more convinced that it was the dreadful conditions of the dark, damp, dirty tenements which were to blame for most of the disease, drunkenness, and crime of the district. "The sights I saw," he said, "gripped my heart until I felt that I must tell of them or burst."

Tell of them he did, reinforcing and dramatizing his stories with pictures he took himself. The newly invented flashlight was important when, in the small hours of the night, he entered a wide-open saloon or climbed narrow tenement stairs to where a dozen men and women slept on the floor of a single small room. Slouch-hatted and bespectacled, he went about without fear and was never molested. Sometimes he was taken for a doctor and asked for help when there was a brawl or a stabbing. His newspaper warned him to "write the facts and spare the comments," but he could not; he felt it all too deeply.

With people moving in from the country to find work in the city, and with immigrants landing from every ship to seek their fortune in America, there was not enough housing in New York to go around. Tenement owners found they could get high rents for even the poorest places. Greedy landlords discovered that they could make even more money by maintaining a no-repairs, no-improvements, pay-or-get-out policy. To help pay the high rent, tenants took in lodgers, singly or by whole families. This made bad conditions worse; sickness increased, and so did suicides and murders. To add to the problem, the door of the corner saloon was always open, inviting discouraged men and women to drown their troubles in drink.

New York's lower East Side speculators erected tall buildings where gardens once had flourished behind pleasant homes. These "rear tenements" had a minimum of light and air and sanitary necessities. Often they were higher than the old houses in front, which owners had subdivided and added stories to in order to take in more people. Tenants even lived in cellars, and some basements were turned into cruller bakeries — fire hazards which imperiled hundreds when the boiling fat caught fire, as often happened.

Jacob Riis felt sympathy for the underpaid workers who lived from hand to mouth, paying more for everything because they could buy only a little at a time. They were caught in a vicious circle, with the wolf always at their door. Riis's heart went out, too, to the overworked and often sickly women who were trying to raise families under impossible conditions. But his greatest concern was for the children, who, he felt, were the slum's most pathetic victims. Their bodies were weakened by lack of nourishing food, and often they turned into thieves from sheer necessity. "The gang," said Riis, "is the ripe fruit of the tenement-house growth." As he watched slum life making criminals of children he declared, "The rescue of the children is the key to the problem of city poverty."

New York's worst slum was the Bend, at the turn of Mulberry Street. Riis called it a pigsty unfit for human habitation. He had the figures to prove that it not only corrupted children; it murdered babies. In its rear tenements one out of every five infants died. The Bend, said Riis, must go — and he said it with set jaw.

It went, though it took nearly ten years, with Jacob Riis almost singlehandedly leading the fight against greedy landlords, dishonest politicians, and an indifferent public. "I was bound to kill The Bend, because it was bad," he wrote years later. "I wanted the sunshine let in there so that it might shine on the children at play . . . joyless children do not make good men." His dream came true as Mulberry Street Park replaced the Bend, providing a pleasant little breathing space for tired adults and restless children. "The place that had been redolent of crime and murder," Riis commented, "became the most orderly in the city."

Long before this happened, Riis began to lecture in churches on slum conditions in an effort to rouse the public which seemed to remain indifferent in spite of his newspaper stories. He illustrated his talk with slides made from pictures he had taken. People were aghast at what they saw and heard. Then the editor of *Scribner's* magazine invited Riis to write an article for the Christmas (1889) issue. He called it "How the Other Half Lives," and the interest in it was so great that he was asked to expand the article into a book.

Jacob Riis wrote this first book of his at night, dead tired after the hard day's work. But in its pages were no weary words. His whole soul went into his writing, along with an unbelievable array of facts gathered from years of firsthand experience on Mulberry Street. The book, also called *How the Other Half Lives,* was an immediate success. It went into several editions and reached many thousands of people, opening their eyes to realities they had never even

suspected. It helped along Riis's "battle with the slums" as
nothing else could have done.

One important result of the book's publication was the
friendship it brought with Theodore Roosevelt. A card with
his signature, left on Riis's desk one day, said simply, "I
have read your book and want to help." From the start, the
two men were like brothers. When the young, vigorous
Roosevelt was made city police commissioner under the
reform administration which Riis had helped to bring in, he
and Riis were often together. Sometimes they toured slum
areas after midnight to check on police activity — or inac-
tivity. They looked into tenement overcrowding and other
conditions which needed correction. More than anyone
else, Jacob Riis helped the young commissioner understand
the problems of the poor and how to deal with them. Later,
when Roosevelt was Governor of New York, he occasionally came down from Albany to visit with Riis factory and
tenement firetraps and rooms where piecework was done —
the "sweatshops" of the garment industry. From Riis,
Theodore Roosevelt learned that "the slum is a problem not
only of government, but of humanity."

All through the "gay nineties," half a century before
Franklin Roosevelt brought "ill-housed, ill-clad, ill-nourished" humanity into national prominence, Jacob Riis was
spending his days and nights fighting to win "freedom from
want" for the poor of New York. All they needed was a
chance, he said — a chance for decent housing at a price
they could pay; a chance for jobs with reasonable hours and
fair wages; a chance to be treated like human beings.
According to Riis, the poor lacked not the instinct but the
opportunity for a better way of life.

Riis had moved his family from Brooklyn to a modest home in Richmond Hills, a little way out on Long Island. One day his small daughters brought him a big bunch of daisies they had picked in the fields nearby and asked him to "take them to the poors." Riis carried the daisies on the Fulton Street ferry across to Manhattan, then gave them away as he walked up Mulberry Street to his office. The outstretched arms, the hunger for beauty among the tenement people who had so little of it in their lives touched him and confirmed his faith in them. He wrote a little story about it in his paper, now the *Evening Sun*. After telling of the response to his gift of daisies, he offered to distribute any flowers other suburban dwellers might want to bring or send him. Flowers came in quantities, flooding his office with their fragrance. Policemen helped him carry them to central points in the neighborhood for distribution. They noticed with wonder, he reported, that "the worst street became suddenly good and neighborly."

The basic solution to the problem of the slums, Riis knew, was nothing so simple as bringing in flowers. He begged the authorities to tear down the crime and disease breeding tenement houses which made the tenants "shiftless, destructive, and stupid," and in their place to give the people decent homes to live in. Plant small parks and playgrounds in congested neighborhoods, he urged. Improve the school system and replace the dark, overcrowded, rat-infested schools with light, modern buildings. Encourage immigrants to learn the language of their new country. Education, said Riis, was "the first and only cure for the poverty problem" — education not only of children but of adults, not only of tenants but of landlords.

More than once Theodore Roosevelt offered his Danish-American friend a post of some importance, first in the state, then in the national Government. But Riis shied away from anything savoring of politics, though he was always willing to serve on city and state commissions and committees which might improve slum conditions. He worked on them vigorously to get small parks and playgrounds in crowded areas, to expose fire-law violations and have the conditions corrected, to investigate sweatshops and do away with child labor. He helped reorganize the police courts and close the police lodging houses where inexperienced youths slept on filthy boards next to hardened criminals — as he himself once had done. In their place he worked to set up farms for vagrants and truant schools for homeless boys. One year he served as general agent of the Council of Good Government Clubs, broadening its aims and accomplishments. Social settlement houses were beginning to appear in congested city districts, and Jacob Riis was honored by having one of them named for him — the Riis Neighborhood House.

As he became better known through his magazine articles and his books, Jacob Riis was increasingly in demand as a lecturer. He traveled across the country, filling halls in cities and towns. His audiences liked the lively, yet earnest way he presented the drab, painful subject of poverty. He could lighten a pathetic story with a touch of humor, being first grave, then gay. Facts were his weapons, and he had a whole arsenal of them at his command. He used them well, backing them up with figures and lightening them with stories from his own experience.

At the end of the century Riis gave up his newspaper job

to have more time for lecturing and writing. Readers found his autobiography, *The Making of an American,* both entertaining and informative, for its pages held "the thrill and throb of life." In them he expressed his love of his native land of Denmark and his delight in the occasional visits he paid there, but he made it plain that he loved his adopted land of America even more and that nothing he could do for her was too much. Jacob Riis's love for people and his compassion for humanity shone through the pages of *The Making of an American* as it did through everything he wrote or said or did. He was able to translate this compassion into effective language and action because, as his friend Lincoln Steffens said, he had "imagination to reconstruct, emotion to suffer, and a kind, fighting spirit to weep, whoop, laugh, and demand."

The last few years of Jacob Riis's life were plagued with heart attacks brought on by overwork, overtravel, overfatigue. But his zest for life and his vision of helping make a better world for others would not let him stop. Many mourned him when he died at sixty-five. People both humble and great spoke of the wrongs he had helped right and of the changes for the better he had brought about. Some, like Frances Perkins, credited him with their decision to devote their lives to social betterment. But of all the many tributes paid Jacob Riis, he would perhaps have liked best that of his great friend Theodore Roosevelt: "He was the most useful American of his day."

Higher wages, shorter working hours, better working conditions.

First American Labor Leader

Samuel Gompers *(1850–1924)*

LIKE JACOB RIIS, Samuel Gompers was born overseas. But instead of coming to America alone at twenty-one, he came with his family when he was thirteen. At ten, as the oldest son he had been taken out of school and put to work, because his father's earnings as a cigarmaker could not support the family. Sam was apprenticed first to a shoemaker, then to a cigarmaker. At fourteen, he could roll tobacco leaves into a fine cigar as deftly as his father.

The Gompers family had lived in the poorest section of London, its East Side. In New York, too, they lived in the poorest section, *its* East Side. Sam worked with his father in the small family flat at their trade of cigarmaking. Together they earned barely enough for the family to get along on. All day Sam worked at the dreary, painstaking task, then at night rushed out eagerly to explore the city. Very soon, he said later, he "learned its customs and found its opportunities." These included night school, free lectures, and a boys' club. He made friends easily and enjoyed their companionship. Presently he was made president of a debating society.

The 1860's were years of change in New York. The day of the craftsman who followed a single product through from start to finish was about over; the era of big industry was beginning, and New York was one of its great centers. Business methods were not yet established. Factories were run in a hit-or-miss fashion, with little attention paid to such things as lighting, sanitation, safety, or health. The relationship between management and labor was usually whatever the "boss" wanted to make it. Most of the time there was work enough to go around, but with so many immigrants arriving from overcrowded Europe and wanting jobs, unscrupulous employers found it easy to lengthen hours and cut wages. When business was bad, they fired their employees without a second thought.

As a child in London, Sam Gompers had seen neighbors who were silkworkers lose their jobs when silkmaking machines were introduced. He never forgot the sight of those discouraged, despairing men trudging about the streets, looking hopelessly for work and wondering how to keep their families from starving. "Unemployment," he said later, with sure knowledge, "is the great horror of a workman with a family dependent upon him."

Young Sam Gompers and his friends on New York's East Side talked a great deal about the problems of the working people — low wages, long hours, poor working conditions, unemployment, insecurity. These things, Sam felt deeply, were dead wrong. To end them — to free workingmen and their families from poverty and exploitation — began to seem to young Sam Gompers the most important thing in the world.

Sam's father belonged to the cigarmakers union, and Sam joined, too. Like other trade unions at this time, it was a small, weak affair which did little for its members. Men and women worked at whatever pay they were offered and under whatever conditions existed. When their wages were cut to an impossibly low point, or when working conditions became too bad or hours too long to be endured, some worker, bolder than the others, would call a strike. Refusing to work was the only way the men saw of bettering their condition. All the men in the factory — sometimes all in a certain trade — would pick up their tools (they usually had to buy their own) and walk out behind the strikeleader. The unions did not direct the strike or have funds to help the men while they were not working, and the workmen themselves had no savings because their wages were so low. They could only hope that the employer's need of their work was great enough to make the strike a success and give them at least some of the things they asked for. Sometimes this happened. More often it didn't. Then, after weeks or months of unemployment, the striking men were forced by hunger and mounting debts to find another job somewhere or go back to the old one — if the employer would take them back — perhaps at even less pay than they had had before.

Sam Gompers grew up in this insecure kind of working world. At sixteen, he quit rolling cigars with his father at home and went to work in a factory — a dingy, dusty loft. The men there, all older than he was, noticed that he talked easily and well and asked him to be their spokesman to try to get the "boss" to improve certain working conditions. When Sam started to speak, the employer was angry. What did he mean, pretending to represent men old enough to be his father? Sam answered that the men could have chosen anyone, but since they had chosen him, he would like to say what they had asked him to say. And he presented their case so well that the employer calmed down and agreed to make the improvements the men wanted.

At seventeen, Sam married an attractive girl a few months younger than himself; she also worked in a factory. For a while they lived with his family, then they established their own small home. Children came, and Sam, though he was a good worker, had his hands full providing for them. But in spite of growing family responsibilities, he never lost sight of his dream. He had, he said, a "passion for bettering men's lives." The plight of workingmen being taken advantage of by their employers angered him, and he said, "I fairly yearned for a stronger labor movement in order that greater justice and opportunities might come into the lives of the world's workers."

To learn how best to help bring this about, young Sam Gompers read everything he could lay his hands on about the labor movements in other countries and in the United States. He went to meetings, to lectures, to debates, and he discussed labor problems with every knowledgeable person interested enough to talk with him.

Rolling cigars was dull work, even though it required some skill. To relieve the monotony, it was the custom in many cigarmaking factories to have one of the workers read aloud, usually articles from labor papers. The listeners would contribute enough finished cigars to make up the difference in the reader's output. Young Gompers was a favorite reader as his voice was clear and strong. To his delight, the articles he selected to read often started a lively discussion and brought out many widely different points of view. Many workers were influenced by the writers and speakers on labor problems who held radical views on how to correct the bad conditions. They sincerely believed that revolutionary methods were required, even an entirely different type of society or form of government.

Sam Gompers recognized these ardent reformers as dreamers, entirely out of step with everyday life. He listened to all of them and gave every theory careful consideration. Then, being a practical, down-to-earth kind of man, he rejected all radical, remote, impractical solutions to the laboring man's problems. The best way to help his fellow workers, he decided, was to gain for them concrete, everyday improvements, such as better wages, shorter hours, and improved working conditions. And the best way to win these goals was to build up the trade unions to a position strong enough to give workingmen the power to insist on their rights. To accomplish this became Sam Gompers's consuming passion.

The year 1873 brought a great depression. Factories closed their doors, turning thousands of workingmen onto the streets. They went from shop to shop, trying in vain to find work. The cold of winter caused intense suffering. Families had no food; heartless landlords turned people without rent money onto the street. Gompers, a naturally kind and sensitive man, reacted keenly to the suffering and need he saw around him. It was not enough, he realized, for a person to do what he could as an individual; people must work together. With a few trusted friends he organized a mass meeting at which it was proposed that the city management take three emergency measures. These were: to create employment through public works; to provide at least a week's maintenance money for the needy; and to prohibit eviction of the unemployed. To Gompers's disappointment, the city management was not interested in any of them.

Some labor leaders called an outdoor meeting of the unemployed. Partly through misunderstanding, partly through fear of a mob, city police were ordered to disperse the crowd. They acted brutally, smashing heads and maiming bodies. Gompers, an onlooker, escaped injury by jumping down an open cellarway. He was angered and dismayed by the affair, but it convinced him that help for the working people would not come either through radical leaders or from the city Government. It must come from the rank and file of the workers themselves, standing together to insist on their rights as human beings. And he plunged again into the task of achieving his dream through strengthening trade unions.

He began with his own area group, or local, of the

cigarmakers union. Like other unions it was not much more
than a glorified debating society, completely unable to cope
with existing economic conditions. Gompers soon became
its president and persuaded its members to plan a progressive program. They agreed to work against wage cuts,
against the tenement-house sweatshop system, and against
factory hazards to health. With other devoted workers
Gompers helped combine all the New York cigarmakers
unions into a federated body dedicated to a continuous
effort to secure for every person in the trade "an existence
worthy of human beings." He got the locals to raise dues to
support the federation and each other, so that a fund could
be built up for sickness, accident, and unemployment relief.

As an enthusiastic, patriotic American, Gompers insisted
that not only were better conditions essential for working
people; they were also of importance to the country. If
America were to remain a democracy, workers must be
able to live decently, for "a starved people have neither the
capacity for, nor interest in, the slow, arduous problems of
self government."

In the years that followed, Gompers fairly lived for the
union. Family life, personal advancement, recreation —
everything fell before the union's struggle to win for laboring people living wages, reasonable working hours, fair
treatment. "The story of the hardships, the laborious toil,
the sacrifices of those early days can never be told," he
wrote years later. "We fought for each gain and with bare
hands unaided carried off victories against the protest of a
hostile world."

Being a union leader, Gompers found, made him unpopular with many people. The heads of the great industries were nearly all opposed to the consolidation of labor forces; it was easier to deal with unorganized workers. The general public seemed to feel no great responsibility to help solve labor's problems. Even the Government, Gompers thought, was indifferent and sometimes antagonistic. Yet he persisted in his struggle "for a little more money — penny by penny; for a little more leisure — minute by minute; for a little more leeway — rule by rule."

In the winter of 1877, a protest strike was called against pay reductions, miserable working conditions, and especially against tenement-house "sweating." It was a disastrous failure. Families had no savings and the unions did not have enough funds to see the strike through. When starvation level was reached, the wage earners crept back to whatever jobs they could find and the strike crumbled away. But from the experience Gompers and other labor leaders learned principles and techniques that were helpful in future strikes.

Sam Gompers's intelligent, dedicated service to labor in the city of New York broadened into state activity. At a state labor convention a plan of benefits which he suggested was adopted. He was asked to go to a town to encourage woolen-mill workers who were having a hard time after striking against a ten per cent wage reduction. Gompers was moved both by their distress and by their spirit, but he could not find a way to keep the strike from failing or the workers from having to return to work at the lower pay rate. Experiences like this led him to spend hours with other New York leaders "thinking, dreaming, discussing, planning." The need which seemed to all of them most urgent

was for a national organization which would band trade
unions together for the help and protection of all.

At last, in 1881, the first national meeting of labor men
of all trades was held in Pittsburgh. Thirty-one-year-old
Sam Gompers told there of what had been done in the New
York cigarmakers union to make it a model for other trade
unions. Appointed to the Committee on Permanent Organization, he helped set up a platform for the new national
body. This platform included such advanced ideas as compulsory education laws, the prohibition of labor of children
under fourteen, factory sanitation and safety provisions,
and a national eight-hour law. Gompers spoke movingly on
child labor, telling of "little children of six, seven, and eight
years of age seated in the middle of a room on the floor, in
all the dirt and dust, stripping tobacco. . . . They began
before daylight and worked till long after dark. Often they
would be overcome with weariness and want of sleep and
fall over upon the tobacco heap. Shame upon us," cried
Gompers, "if we do not raise our voices against such
crimes!" Unanimously the convention adopted an anti-child-
labor resolution.

Gompers was an active leader of the new national organization during the several years of its existence. Among
other things, he edited a four-page trade-union paper. For
years he had been a forceful speaker; now he learned also
to write forcefully. The paper's slogan was a concise statement of his ambitions for labor: "Higher wages, shorter
working hours, better working conditions."

The federation was not strong enough to cope with the
problems it faced — centralized industrial management, internal strife, and the competition of another, rather imprac-

tical labor organization, the Knights of Labor. Gompers agreed with other trade-union heads that it would be wise to create an entirely new national organization. This was done in 1886, and Samuel Gompers was elected the first president of the American Federation of Labor.

A thousand-dollar salary was all the Federation could offer. The organization was poor because its constituents were wage earners, and poor. "It has always been the poor who have helped the poor," said Mr. Gompers optimistically. He was convinced that by working together they would bring about better conditions. In spite of the salary being considerably less than he was earning, he could not resist the challenge of heading the new national organization.

Like most of his friends, Gompers had no property or savings. His family endured privations along with him to help him fulfill his dream. They had almost no changes of clothing and only one pair of shoes apiece; Gompers had to wear his slippers at the office while his shoes were being repaired. But neither poverty nor ceaseless toil could depress him, for he was "full of fire and dreams" and an "inextinguishable desire" to help his fellows.

The first office of the American Federation of Labor was in one small room, furnished with makeshift desk and chairs, and files made from old boxes. With no money for a typewriter, Gompers wrote his letters longhand, as well as the monthly paper he got out, for which his young son addressed the wrappers. Gompers's work was his life. After a busy day in the office he often went out to speak at labor meetings or to confer with other labor leaders. He also traveled as far as the money on hand would take him, to help organize unions, advise about collective bargaining and strikes, and "establish the name and service of the American Federation of Labor in national labor circles." His ability, his earnestness, and his liking for people won him the goodwill of workers everywhere and soon made the A.F. of L. a force in the industrial world as "the unified activity of the trade union men." Yet, made up as it was of self-governing national unions, one only to each trade, which in turn were made up of local unions, the A.F. of L. itself had no real authority.

For several years Samuel Gompers was the only full-time official of the Federation. As his accomplishments multiplied and the strength of the organization grew, he met with increasingly bitter opposition from industrial heads and "big business." Often he was shadowed by men trying to catch him in some misstep so that they could weaken his influence or even destroy him. But opposition only made him more persistent in his lifelong campaign for social justice.

One matter which worried him was the large number of socialists and anarchists who found their way into the trade unions. In a free organization all shades of opinion could be expected, and it was inevitable that radical thinkers would try to influence, even control, the unions and their Federation. But Gompers refused to let the A. F. of L. become the tool of idealists, socialists, or anarchists. He hated violence and fought to keep the labor movement clear of it. Contracts were to be kept, and collective bargaining to be used, with strikes resorted to only when negotiation failed.

Gompers stood up for human rights to the last ditch. He considered injunctions against picketing or open-air speech-making a violation of the right of free speech and assemblage. Convinced that his position was just and constitutional, he risked any consequences. "I hold a jail more roomy in the expression of my judgment and convictions," he said, "than would be the whole world if I were to submit to repression and be denied the right to express myself." By showing this sort of courage he helped West Virginia miners win their strike. When a judge unsympathetic to labor sentenced him to prison for ignoring an injunction and Gompers had to endure seven years of litigation with the sentence hanging over his head, he could still joke. "Prison holds no terrors for me," he said. "My fare cannot be simpler. My bed cannot be plainer. And the rest might do me good."

Gompers was much opposed to affiliating the A. F. of L. with any political party, though he believed in using political means wherever it would help the cause of labor. Through his constructive, realistic though unsensational program, the organization grew steadily. For every year except one he was its president; that year a Socialist defeated him and he spent the time traveling, organizing unions for the United Garment Workers to improve "the deplorable conditions" of that industry's "persecuted and downtrodden workers."

In 1897, the American Federation of Labor moved its headquarters to Washington to keep in closer touch with national legislative proceedings. With expansion of the organization, Samuel Gompers had become a national figure. This neither brought him wealth nor made him "pull his punches." He spoke out against the illegal ways by which he believed financiers and business corporations were control-

ling elections, courts, and congressional actions. He blasted
judges and politicians who favored property rights over
human rights and who turned the antitrust law against trade
unions.

Years later, Gompers was to hear President Wilson state
the belief which he (Gompers) had spent thirty years trying
to get across to legislators and executives, even Presidents:
"A man's labor is not a commodity but a part of his life."

With a smile Gompers admitted, "It takes fortitude to
continue hammering away at a project year after year." But
Gompers was a "hammering" kind of man. Tactfully but
persistently he kept on resisting injunctions in industrial
disputes and treating labor unions as if they came within the
scope of the antitrust law. Labor scored a triumph when the
Government created a Department of Labor, with its Secretary added to the President's Cabinet. Another triumph
came when Gompers's phrase was written into labor law:
"The labor of a human being is not a commodity or article
of commerce."

With World War I, the labor movement came into its
own. Gompers abandoned his ideas of pacifism. He withdrew from publication a book made up of articles he had
written on peace, which the Carnegie Endowment for International Peace was bringing out. When President Wilson
appointed him to the Advisory Commission to the Council
of National Defense, he offered the wholehearted cooperation of labor and in a fervent spirit of patriotism organized
the country's labor front to meet production needs for the
duration.

In August of 1918, Gompers went to Europe on a
mission of goodwill for labor. After the peace, President

Wilson appointed him to the Commission on International Labor Legislation, meeting in Paris during the Peace Conference. Gompers was distressed at the differences between Old and New World labor standards, principles, and methods. Back in the States, he supported the peace treaty with all his might, calling attention to its recognition of "the rights, interests, and welfare of the workers." He was dismayed when the Senate failed to ratify it.

In the postwar years Gompers found it difficult to hold for the labor forces the gains they had made during the war years. Both industry and the Government went back on wartime agreements, and management-labor relations deteriorated. Yet each year the American Federation of Labor membership showed a gain; each year public opinion grew more friendly toward labor; each year trade unions were held in higher esteem.

So also was their leader, Samuel Gompers. Never in his *Seventy Years of Life and Labor* — the title of his autobiography written in 1923, the year before his death — had he wavered from his dream of a better life for the workers of America, or given less than his best toward achieving that dream. Always he put the cause of labor above personal advantage. Samuel Gompers died a poor man, but he had brought the laboring men and women of America a long way on their path toward freedom from want and justice for all.

First Children's Bureau Chief

Julia Clifford Lathrop *(1858–1932)*

JANE ADDAMS returned from Europe in the late 1880's, determined to set up in Chicago a settlement house similar to London's Toynbee Hall. She spoke at various places in an effort to win understanding and cooperation for her project. In her audience at Rockford College was a young woman who had been helping her father in his law office since her graduation from Vassar. Julia Lathrop had a brilliant mind, a pleasant manner, and progressive ideas. Like her father, she believed in civil-service reform, women's rights, and a fairer deal for society's have-nots. It was not surprising that Jane Addams's idea appealed to her strongly.

Julia Lathrop offered to go into Chicago regularly to conduct a club at the new settlement house, which Miss Addams called Hull-House. For a year she did this, becoming well acquainted with the overcrowded, poorly ventilated, unsanitary tenement houses of the neighborhood, with their dark stairways, leaky roofs, and fire hazards. She talked with their occupants, most of them immigrants from Europe, who worked as factory hands and unskilled laborers. She learned firsthand of their long hours of work, their low wages, and their frequent periods of unemployment. She tried to help them lose their forlornness as strangers in a strange land by joining in the Hull-House activities and forming friendships there.

After a year of weekly commuting, Miss Lathrop left her parents' comfortable Rockford home to become a resident at Hull-House. She also became a volunteer visitor for the county agent's office, responsible for investigating charity cases in the ten blocks around Hull-House. At first the men in charge at the office were afraid that the lady might become sentimental about the "poor furriners" and be a sort of "coal chute" for giving away county supplies. They soon changed their minds. Miss Lathrop, they found, looked at problems in a broad and realistic way; her reports were dependable and her advice sound.

Julia Lathrop soon saw the need for new social legislation and for better administration of laws that already existed. The problems of the poor, she realized, should be approached in a more scientific way. She already had a very real appreciation of the management side of the economic picture. Now she was gaining an intimate knowledge of the labor side. Because of this double viewpoint, and a natural moderation, she was an excellent kind of person to play a key part in this beginning era of the new science of sociology. Her scholarly understanding of the overall situation, balanced by a warm sympathy for the individual and his or her troubles and her sense of personal responsibility, were continually driving her into action to correct bad situations.

A business depression and a "winter of panic" followed the great Chicago World's Fair of 1893. People without work, their savings gone, their children hungry, their homes cold, descended on the county agent's office. Their arms ached from holding their market baskets above their heads because of the crowd as they stood, hour after hour, waiting their turn to get their paltry allowance of food.

Julia Lathrop, as county volunteer visitor, climbed countless rickety steps and descended into scores of dank cellars to explore the cases of direst need. She arranged for food credit, coal delivery, hospital care, burials. One day she discovered that garments were being made, sweatshop fashion, in the tenement homes of diseased persons. With another Hull-House resident she persuaded the Chicago Board of Health to destroy the garments and so avert an almost certain smallpox epidemic. Without regard for her own safety, she visited the patients in the contagious hospital and carried messages from them to their families and from their families to them. Altogether, it was a winter she never forgot.

That same year Miss Lathrop began her work as a

member of the Illinois State Board of Charities. Still living at Hull-House, she traveled all over Illinois, inspecting state poorhouses, county farms, children's orphanages and industrial schools, infirmaries and hospitals, insane asylums and homes for the feebleminded. She was appalled by the amount of political corruption in the state. Many institution superintendents had been appointed by politicians in return for some favor, with no regard at all for personal qualifications. Often there was not even an interview or examination. Miss Lathrop fought against this patronage system. She knew it was useless to attack these injustices head-on, so she used diplomacy, recommending to politicians appointment on the basis of civil service and merit. She emphasized that the recovery, perhaps even the lives, of the people in the state institutions depended upon the interest and skill of those who cared for them. Because of her friendly approach and constructive helpfulness, some of the institution superintendents gained the sense of responsibility they had lacked and really tried to improve conditions.

For four years, from 1901 to 1905, Illinois politics were so bad that Miss Lathrop refused to serve on the board. Then, disturbed by the needs and hopeful of making improvements, she returned to this work for several more years. In spite of much political opposition, she managed to accomplish a good deal.

Public indifference to the conditions in public institutions troubled Miss Lathrop even more than political corruption. She talked to women's clubs and other organizations all over the state in an effort to interest the people of Illinois in improving the institutions for which they were indirectly responsible. She told them of the appalling conditions in many of these places — of fire hazards in some, bad food and insufficient heat in others, cruelty in a few, and neglect in many. She stressed the importance of better training for nurses and attendants, of introducing occupational therapy in mental hospitals, of encouraging mental hygiene, and of separating feebleminded children from the chronically insane. She became so interested in the treatment of the mentally ill that she went to Scotland and Belgium in 1898 to study their methods.

Concerned as she was for these unfortunates, she was even more concerned for the nation's children. Whenever she was at Hull-House she was always involved with the activities and problems of the neighborhood young people and children. She was genuinely fond of them; she understood their language, their humor, their interests, and she had an effective way of encouraging them to be and do their best.

Julia Lathrop's interest in children and young people extended far beyond the Hull-House neighborhood. She was concerned about the amount of child labor in factories and on farms all over the country. She was concerned about the health of children, about their education, and about the way society treated them when they got into trouble.

It was quite usual for children who had committed some minor crime to be housed in detention homes or jails along with seasoned criminals and then to be judged in the same court. If delinquent children were over ten, they were tried in police courts. If they were convicted, they were usually fined. Then, if the parents were either too poor or too unconcerned to pay the fine, as often happened, the children were sent to city prison. If a kindhearted justice, hating to see this happen, turned them loose, they very often did the same thing over again. If the court minimized the offense to keep the children out of jail, they would be sent to an industrial school and put in with totally innocent children whose only offense was that they were homeless.

Julia Lathrop roused the Chicago Women's Club to install women matrons in police stations and jails, and to start a school for boys awaiting trial. But this was not enough. Largely due to Miss Lathrop, just before the turn of the century the first juvenile court in the world was set up in Chicago. Its basic principle was that "a child that broke the law was to be dealt with by the State as a wise parent would deal with a wayward child." Instead of prosecution and defense, there was an investigation, followed by a discussion and a decision based on what would be best for the child. The juvenile court eventually had its own building, with quarters for the probation department, the detention home, schoolrooms and gymnasium. Julia Lathrop was the first president of the Juvenile Court Committee, responsible for selecting probation officers and for raising money to pay their salaries. Since this was a totally new field, the committee had to rely on their knowledge of human nature in making appointments. The number of repeaters in the court indicated that many of the children were psychopathic cases. So a clinic was set up in charge of a doctor-psychologist accustomed to dealing with children. This first such clinic anywhere developed into the Illinois Institute for Juvenile Research.

Miss Lathrop also helped bring into being the Mothers' Pension Act, administered by the juvenile court to help the dependent child, and a vocational bureau in the public school system. She worked constantly for adequate public playgrounds and parks, and for "a community which consciously protects public health, recreation, and education."

Poverty, Miss Lathrop blamed for most of childhood's troubles. "A large part of juvenile delinquency," she said, "is due to grinding poverty. It is at the basis of our social problems." It would take state action, she believed, to abolish poverty — state action "based upon economics and not upon sentiment."

With her deep devotion to social betterment and her gift for public speaking, Julia Lathrop was able to interest many groups of people in starting much-needed organizations. Among these were the Mental Hygiene Society, the Illinois Immigrants' Protective League, and the Chicago School of Civics and Philanthropy, which became the Graduate School of Social Service Administration of the University of Chicago. Schools for training social workers were also established in New York, Boston, and St. Louis. Even more were needed, Miss Lathrop said, "for giving social work a wide scientific outlook, so that those engaged in it may have the power to see the field as well as the furrow."

Private organizations, like private charity, were too "capricious," Julia Lathrop felt, to supply the steady, reliable service the nation's needy required. This service was a necessary function of Government, and it should be managed in a businesslike, scientific, professional way, with research, studies, and statistics, though without any "loss of heart." She coveted a "big and generous vision" and a "sustained intelligent public interest" to promote "the enlistment of the finest trained ability in the public service" and to keep that service free from political interference.

In 1910 and 1911, Julia Lathrop and her sister made a trip around the world. She returned, said her friend Jane Addams, "with a poignant knowledge of the bitter poverty in which so large a portion of the world population lives. . . . The journey itself added an historic background and a wider understanding to her long experience in dealing with the helpless, with the poor, and with those handicapped in mind and body."

The next year President Taft set up the Children's Bureau and appointed Julia Lathrop its first chief. Incidentally, she was the first woman to head a federal bureau. It was the "first expression of the nation's care for all the interests of all children," and its purpose was "to investigate and report upon all matters pertaining to the welfare of children and child life among all classes of our people."

In other hands, the Children's Bureau might have been "an insignificant agency of petty reform," but not in Miss Lathrop's. In spite of its lack of power and of money, under her leadership it became an important influence in decreasing infant and maternal mortality, in abolishing child labor, and in improving the care of dependent, delinquent, and defective children. The new chief kept her eye on the possibilities, rather than the limitations of her office. She set out on a course of investigating, then reporting the facts to the nation. While part of her carefully picked staff did scientific research, others produced bulletins, charts, cartoons, and news releases.

Infant and maternal mortality was the first problem the Children's Bureau tackled. Why was it that the death rate for typhoid, diphtheria, tuberculosis, and pneumonia had declined but not mothers' deaths in childbirth? And why did

fourteen civilized countries lose fewer mothers than the
United States? Children's Bureau studies proved it was
because of the lack of proper hygiene and skilled care. The
answer? The bureau recommended that every city and town
provide instructional services for expectant mothers, and
every county set up a health-training center, coordinating
the efforts of doctors, teachers, and social workers.

Why did one out of every eight American babies die in
its first year — in some parts of the country one out of
every three? And why did ten civilized countries have a
lower infant mortality rate than the United States? The
Children's Bureau showed that this appalling waste of life
was due to "poverty, ignorance, and social maladjustment."
Many more babies of very poor families died than of
families where the fathers earned a more adequate income.
The Children's Bureau publicized the relation of infant
mortality to income, housing congestion, sanitation, and
employment of mothers before and after babies' births. Miss
Lathrop campaigned for more public-health nurses and
headed an educational campaign which sparked the opening of hundreds of baby centers for weighing and measuring
and other tests.

A duty of the Children's Bureau was to report on all
legislation affecting children. Its tabulation, begun with
mothers'-pension and child-labor laws, revealed the lack of
national vital statistics and the wide differences in state
laws, though the basic needs of all children were the same.
Often there were even inconsistencies within the same state.
At Miss Lathrop's suggestion, many Governors set up commissions to review state laws concerning children. Child
welfare, she pointed out, "is and should remain a state and

local responsibility, while social research as a concern of the Government provides a free stream of useful knowledge."

During the First World War the Children's Bureau was charged with caring for dependents of enlisted men, for soldiers' compensations and insurance, and for the children of war-working mothers. Again Miss Lathrop journeyed to Europe, this time to see how other countries at war were handling their child-welfare problems. She was impressed by their insistence on protecting the children in order to safeguard the future. On her return she urged Americans to hold on to the hard-won child-protection laws which were threatened by the war. She begged them not to allow mothers and children to die needlessly through poverty and civic neglect, or to permit the children to grow up "ignorant, weak, unskilled, unhappy." How much better to keep children well than to wait to cure them; to educate them than to send them to work too early; and to set up juvenile courts than to force delinquent children into the criminal category!

In 1919, the Children's Bureau sponsored a Children's Year to make the American people more conscious of child welfare as a national and local problem. Regional conferences were held, and newspaper and magazine articles written to arouse people to the need for "public protection of childhood at home, at play, and at work." The "irreducible minimum standards" set up by the bureau included public protection of the health of mothers and children through maternity-, infant-, and child-health centers, clinics, school hygiene, and recreational facilities; a sixteen-year minimum age for leaving school; and state supervision for defectives, delinquents, and dependents.

"Let's give them all a fair start!" Miss Lathrop urged. The basic problem, she still insisted, was poverty. "Statistics show that infant mortality lessens as wages of fathers increase," and "The enfeebled in mind or body are found in overwhelming proportion among those whose lives are most barren of comfort and knowledge and financially on the lowest level." The answer, Julia Lathrop claimed, lay in two words — "Abolish poverty." This was the surest way to lessen the "social wastage" of dependency, delinquency, and defect. Children, she said, "are not safe or happy if their parents are miserable, and parents must be miserable if they cannot protect a home against poverty. The power to maintain a decent family living standard is the primary essential of child welfare."

When, after ten years of service, Julia Lathrop left the Children's Bureau in 1921, her name was said to be "synonomous with child welfare in the United States." Certainly she had set new standards for the public protection of childhood and had led the country a long way toward achieving them. The evils of child labor were largely done away with, infant mortality had declined, and children's chances of growing into healthy maturity were greatly improved.

Miss Lathrop continued to work for child welfare in the less strenuous later years of her life. She was in demand as a lecturer and, in 1923 — still linking health and delinquency problems to want, and still optimistic — she publicly gave an affirmative answer to the question "Can we abolish poverty within fifty years?" She had worked to secure the vote for women; now she urged them to accept greater responsibility in education and politics. In 1925, her work and influence became international in scope when she was appointed to the Advisory Child Welfare Committee of the League of Nations.

At Julia Lathrop's death, a decade after her retirement from the Children's Bureau, Jane Addams called her "one of the most useful women in the whole country." She was credited with "statesmanlike vision, ability to work out careful plans, and the patience to carry through constructive programs."

Of greater importance was her natural human sympathy. It was this which, coupled with her deep sense of "community consciousness," broadened into a lifelong effort to improve the chances, not only of sick or orphaned or wayward or helpless children, but of all the nation's children to "a fair start in life."

To help the man furthest down.

Southern Plant Wizard

George Washington Carver
(1864–1943)

A SMALL dark-skinned boy squat-
ted beside a patch of finely
raked soil in the shade of the
Ozark oaks. With sensitive fingers
he loosened the earth around the
roots of a sickly looking plant, then
carefully examined the other plants
he had brought to this private little
garden of his. Some of them had
been discarded by neighbors; some he had dug up in nearby
fields or forest. He pruned drooping leaves, moved one
plant to a shady spot, and put another in a brighter place.

As he worked, he crooned a song in a strangely shrill little voice.

His gardening done, the boy picked up his basket and went farther into the woods to search for fruits and flowers, mosses and barks. Already, at eight or nine, George knew which plants were good for cooking, for medicines, or for dyes. These he would take home to Aunt Sue Carver; the others he would add to his own little garden or to his treasure pile behind the barn.

George and Jim were children of a gentle Negro woman who had been the well-loved slave of the Carvers, a kindly, hard-working German immigrant couple who owned several acres of the rich Missouri land. In the fearful days that followed the Civil War, the Negro woman had been stolen by raiders and never heard of again, but her baby, taken with her and abandoned by the roadside, had been rescued for the price of a horse. Sick with the croup, suffering from shock and exposure, baby George grew slowly into a frail, stammering child. Jim, his husky older brother, helped farmer Carver. George was better at household tasks — cooking and cleaning, making butter, tending the chickens and the dooryard garden. Because of his magic way with growing things, neighbors brought him their sickly plants to heal; they called him the "little plant doctor." Though his speech was slow, his eyes were bright and observant and his movements quick. Too bad, said Mrs. Carver, that such a smart boy could not go to school, but as everyone knew, only white children went to the school at Diamond Grove. She gave George an old spelling book; he pored over it until he knew its every word and letter.

At ten, fearful but determined to learn, George set off for

the nearest school for colored children. It was in Neosho, eight miles away. He found a home nearby with the Watkinses, a childless Negro couple who treated him like a son. George repaid them by cooking, cleaning, washing and ironing, and making their garden flourish. For three years he lived with them, attending the crowded one-room school along with seventy-five other colored children and absorbing eagerly whatever knowledge the poorly trained teacher could pass on to him. Then, reluctantly leaving his foster family, he traveled to Fort Scott, Kansas, where he had heard that schools were better. To earn his keep and to pay for his books, he worked as a family's "hired girl," as cook in a hotel, as a launderer, and at harvesttime at bundling wheat in the fields. He was growing into a tall, agreeable lad of sinewy strength.

From one small Kansas town to another George Carver moved as opportunities opened and as he needed better schools. Wherever he was, he found time to roam the fields and woods in search of lovely flowers and unfamiliar plants. Entranced with some flower paintings he saw, he attempted to draw flowers himself. Whenever the school he was attending had an art class he was sure to be in it. He was poor at copying scenes and objects, but astonishingly good at painting flowers. Music delighted him almost as much as art; he bought and learned to play a mouth organ and a secondhand accordion.

Everywhere he went, people liked George Carver. They found him capable, friendly, and dependable, and with a passion for learning. Never did he indulge in self-pity, though he was often sad at the thought of his lost mother and his brother Jim, dead from smallpox. He celebrated his graduation from high school by paying a visit to the Carvers and Watkinses. They were enormously proud of the tall lad and thrilled with his news that he was going on to college; that he had been accepted at the college in Highland, Kansas.

In September, George Carver presented himself in the college president's office. The official took one look at his dark skin, then announced coldly, "We don't take Negroes here."

Stunned, George turned and without a word walked out of the room, the building, the campus. Gone were his dreams, his plan to climb farther and farther up the ladder of knowledge and then to use that knowledge to serve others of his race less fortunate than he.

He took a job as a picker in a fruit orchard on the outskirts of town. He did not stay long. The United States Government had recently opened land in western Kansas for homesteading. George went out there, took up a claim, built himself a soddy, and tried to develop a farm. But it was grazing, not farming land. He worked for a neighboring rancher and roamed over the wide plains, fascinated by this different kind of country. Days and nights under the great sky helped to heal his wounded spirit. During the winter blizzards he painted, created designs, and made lace. And he studied, for his dreams refused to leave him. Sometime, somewhere, somehow he would find a way to fulfill them.

He missed trees and streams, grass and flowers — and people. Long before his five-year homesteading term was up he traveled east to Iowa, carrying his few belongings, half a dozen cactus plants, and a pocketful of rock and mineral

specimens. Along the way he did odd jobs. Finding living
cheap and work plentiful in Winterset, Iowa, he became the
chef at the hotel, then set up a laundry in a cottage at the
edge of town. In his free time he walked in the woods,
delighting in the lush vegetation.

A friendly family he met in church invited him to their
home. The wife, a musician, noticed George's admiration of
the piano and offered to give him lessons in return for help
with her garden. After they came to know him better,
George's new friends encouraged him to go on with his
formal education and to try again to enter a college. They
assured him that Simpson College, in Indianola, Iowa, had
no color bias.

With many misgivings George walked the twenty-five
miles there and hesitantly applied for admission. He was
made welcome; faculty and students were friendly; the
classes were a delight to him. When the students learned
that George would do laundry and mending to earn his
way, the work poured in. He was in demand, too, for
musical performances, for his tasteful fern-and-vine decora-
tions for special events, and for companionable evenings of
friendly talk. Never had he been so happy. Here at last he
was a human being among other human beings, not judged
by his color but accepted for himself. Somewhere along the
line he had added a middle name to prevent confusion with
another George Carver, and from here on he signed himself
George Washington Carver.

His teachers tried to steer him toward practical courses,
but George had his heart set on painting. In the top-floor
art department, painting his beloved flowers, he was in
heaven — just as he was when working with them in

garden or greenhouse. Was this, he sometimes wondered as he walked in the woods on a Sunday, a selfish joy? What had happened to his old dream of bringing knowledge to others of his race?

His art teacher's father was professor of horticulture at Iowa State College at Ames. Through her influence George Washington Carver made a hard decision. Passionately though he loved painting, he knew it was science rather than art that his people in the South needed. With a sigh, he pulled up roots at Simpson and left for Iowa State, to specialize in agriculture.

This much larger college was well advanced in scientific agriculture, with greenhouses, experimental station, and up-to-date equipment. Although he was its first Negro student, George soon felt at home, respected and liked. He worked in the campus greenhouse, made drawings for the college science bulletin and for the state agricultural society, and was in demand by athletic teams to massage strained muscles with his long, sensitive fingers. When he could find time, he painted; several of his flower paintings were sent to the Chicago World's Fair and hung in its art exhibit.

In 1894, he received his B.S. degree and was overjoyed to be invited to remain at Iowa State as a member of its botany department while he worked toward his M.S. As part of his work he traveled through the state giving talks on practical agriculture; he also made a valuable collection of fungi, and he experimented in grafting. His longing to paint still fought with his scientific interest in agriculture, but he loved the daily challenge of his work, the opportunity to develop his "intuitive affinity with nature," and his companionship with like-minded people. The dream of helping his people persisted more vaguely, postponed from year to year.

Suddenly he was faced with the need to make a decision. At Tuskegee, Alabama, the great Negro educator Booker T. Washington had developed a school for Negroes from a one-room, one-teacher affair into a going institution. But its students lacked instruction in scientific farming, the very thing they needed most. They were not much interested; in their minds farming was connected with unhappy, humiliating memories of cotton picking. They wanted to forget it and go on to book learning and trades. But Dr. Washington knew that the whole economy of the South and the chances of the Southern Negroes for a brighter future were tied up in the better use of the soil. At Iowa State College was the man best fitted to head the program he had in mind — George Washington Carver. Dr. Washington determined to bring him to Tuskegee. He wrote Carver, offering him the directorship of a new department of agriculture. The salary was small; the problems were great. So also was the opportunity.

Carver had no choice. This was what he had been preparing himself for, for years. Sadly he prepared to leave Iowa, to embark on the dream he had almost buried in his happy contentment with his work and surroundings. In early October, 1896, his colleagues regretfully bade him farewell. As a remembrance, they presented him with a fine microscope.

As the train bore him farther and farther into the South, Carver's excitement mounted. He had never before seen cotton growing. It was picking time, and in field after field he saw colored men, women, and children, dressed in jeans or ragged skirts, stuffing the white bolls into great burlap sacks. He noted the rickety shacks with the cotton planted right up to the door and no sign of trees or flowers. He saw bare gullied land, trees gone, topsoil washed away, goodness sapped by repeated cotton crops. Carver's heart ached for the people of this sick land. He vowed to put every ounce of strength and skill and knowledge that God had given or would give him into helping cure the land, improve the soil, bring health and ease and beauty to the poor brown drudges of the field.

At Tuskegee, Carver found a campus which was nothing but a stretch of bare yellow ground, broken by deep gullies. A churn stood under a tree, a few sheep and cows and a single yoke of oxen in a nearby field, and a score of razorback hogs in the adjoining pine woods. There were no greenhouses, no gardens, no experimental station — and only thirteen students had signed up for the new course. The Tuskegee president, Dr. Washington, said only, "There is a great deal to be done. How it is done, I leave in your hands. Just one suggestion: Don't mention farming; speak instead of scientific agriculture."

Carver nodded and smiled, a quiet, understanding smile. He recognized this man's ability and faith and could foresee his own admiration for him growing into affection. Already his loyalty was pledged and his head swam with the challenge of the work ahead.

The new professor planned his laboratory on paper and drew sketches of necessary equipment. Then he called his students together, showed them the sketches, and proposed their first adventure. "We will find materials and make these things ourselves," he told them. "Where is the town dump?"

From it and other rubbish heaps, and by asking at back doors for discarded household utensils, the students gathered old bottles which they used for beakers, flatirons to serve as pounders, tins which with holes punched in them could be used to grade soil, an old ink bottle into which they stuck a cord laced with a twisted-string wick for a Bunsen burner. And of course they had Carver's precious microscope. Soon they spoke with pride of their laboratory, and with greater pride of their experiments in scientific agriculture. Every week more students came to study under the soft-spoken, learned professor who had a way of making common things exciting.

From before sunrise to long after dark Professor Carver was busy directing the care of the animals, setting up a dairy, landscaping the school grounds, showing the students how and where to build fences, and teaching classes. They must start an experimental station, he told Dr. Washington, and Dr. Washington was able to get from the state legislature an appropriation of fifteen hundred dollars for it.

The new professor did wonders with the money. He and his students cleared twenty acres of "no-good" land. With a two-horse plow, the first in the region, they worked into it barnyard manure, muck from the swamps, and leaf mold from the woods. The cowpeas they planted came up poorly, but they were not a loss, for Carver had them cooked and served to prove that they made good food for humans as well as for cattle. The next crop was sweet potatoes. These did better, and the cotton crop which followed was the best that had been seen anywhere about for a long time.

Farmers came from miles around to see the Tuskegee farm. They learned from it how rotation of crops rested and enriched the land; how compost piles could take the place of expensive fertilizer — or of no soil enrichment at all; and how erosion could be prevented or corrected. Once a month Professor Carver held an all-day Farmers Institute with everything on display and with him and his students on hand to answer questions, give advice, analyze soils. He also began to issue bulletins which explained fundamental principles of scientific agriculture in the simplest terms and gave recipes for new ways to cook peas, sweet potatoes, and other common vegetables. He called attention to the many weeds — "misplaced plants" he called them — which were rich in vitamins and minerals, freely available for only the trouble of picking, and often possessing not only food but medicinal or other uses. He showed how the fibers of many of them could be turned into string or rope or used to weave mats or rugs.

Every morning Professor Carver was up and out before sunrise. As he studied the abundant natural resources he felt sure that, properly used, they could eliminate poverty in this part of the world. "Use your eyes," he kept telling the students who went with him on his exploratory trips. "Every plant has a purpose; it is our job to discover that purpose. Nothing need be wasted." And he continually proved his point by making useful things from neglected materials. By washing and heating local clays, then reducing them to powder and mixing with oils, he made a whitewash to lighten the inside of dingy cabins and colored paints to brighten the outside. Beauty, he preached, is as important for the spirit as good food for the body. He told his students, "Make your homes attractive inside, and outside, plant flowers." Never did they see him without a flower in his lapel.

To get needed laboratory and farm equipment more

costly than the school could afford, Professor Carver set aside his shyness and dislike of front and went on a concert tour. Night after night, dressed in formal clothes, he played the piano all over the South. Besides earning the needed money, he saw firsthand the appalling conditions under which most of his race were living. The Graham-Lipscomb biography describes them in these words: "hundreds of squalid, ramshackle cabins tenanted by forlorn, emaciated, poverty-stricken Negroes who year after year struggled in cotton fields and disease-laden swamps, trying to eke out a miserable existence."

These were the people Professor Carver felt he must reach! Many of them could not read the bulletins he issued; most of them could not get to Tuskegee; some were too weary to attend his lectures in their neighborhood schools and churches. These people were still planting cotton up to their doorsteps, buying on credit at the local store the "meal, meat, and molasses" which nourished them so inadequately that they went about weak and weary and often suffering from pellagra.

"To help the man furthest down," Professor Carver's fertile brain devised Tuskegee's demonstration wagon and brought it into being. On it were garden tools, a churn, a steel plow, a separator, a cultivator. Each week it carried the professor-scientist and a few of his students into a different part of the region to show farmers the best ways to plow, plant, prune and spray, hatch chickens, preserve meats, cure plant and animal diseases. The wives learned how to churn, to can and pickle surplus foods for winter use, to weave rugs and make curtains. For all of them Professor Carver had free packets of seeds sent to him by his friend James Wilson, the United States Secretary of Agriculture, formerly professor at Iowa State College. "Live at home! Plant vegetables! Keep chickens and pigs! And save five cents a day toward buying your own place!" the Tuskegee professor advised.

Little by little the Alabama Negroes became healthier and more prosperous. They raised more crops. The quantity and quality of their cotton improved. And Tuskegee flourished. Dr. Washington proposed to raise Professor Carver's salary, but he would not accept a penny more than his beginning pay. "What would I do with more money?" he asked. "It would be a bother."

Then came a new menace — the boll weevil. As it crept steadily closer to Alabama, Professor Carver advised farmers not to plant cotton, to plow under the stalks in the fields and then to plant peanuts. Peanuts in place of cotton? It was unthinkable! And so most of the farmers planted cotton as usual. When the boll weevil came and destroyed the entire crop, they remembered the professor's advice and planted peanuts. And so many peanuts ripened that the market could not absorb them all and they were left in the fields to rot.

Professor Carver blamed himself; he was the one who had turned the farmers from cotton to peanuts. He locked himself in his laboratory with a bushel of peanuts and worked day and night. He separated the peanut into its component parts — fats, oils, starches, acids, and so on. Then, always observing the three laws of compatability, temperature, and pressure, he tried different combinations. The result was more than twenty products, including peanut cheese, peanut milk, and peanut butter. The day was saved. Manufacturers became interested in the "lowly pea-nut" when they learned of the many things that could be made from it. Eventually this number rose to more than three hundred, and peanuts became the second cash crop of the South.

From the sweet potato, too, Professor Carver made many things. He showed farmers how to raise two crops a year and, because the vegetable spoiled quickly, how to dry it to grate for flour or for use in other ways. He also experimented with the soybean, and with other plants which held food or industrial possibilities. He reasoned that building up a few native industries would help the South's economy and increase its agricultural prosperity. If farmers would utilize what nature provided, find uses for waste products, adapt and transform natural materials, they could get from their land everything they needed for themselves and in addition supply many raw materials for industry.

Professor Carver arranged to spend less time teaching and more time in his laboratory. The new science he was creating — making wealth from waste through the powers of soil and air and sun and the genius of man — was named "chemurgy," putting chemistry to work. George Washington Carver, the first and greatest chemurgist, not only developed products from the peanut and the sweet potato but also made paints from local clay, paper and wallboard from cotton waste, useful things from nut shells, plant stalks, pine cones, even from sawdust. This unassuming man "opened wide the door to the synthetic kingdom."

Men came from all over the country and from as far away as Australia to talk to Professor Carver and to carry home his ideas. Peanut manufacturers invited him to explain at their meeting the possibilities of the peanut, and then asked him to go to Washington to do the same thing before a Congressional committee, in connection with a protective tariff measure. Dr. Washington was proud of the fame the scientist was bringing to Tuskegee. Professor Carver was proud only of the way he was "turning men back to God's earth for their needs" and helping people become healthier and happier.

Many offers came to him from manufacturing concerns. Thomas Edison promised Carver fame and fortune if he would come to New Jersey to work with him. "Together," said Edison, "we shall unlock the universe." Carver answered simply, "They need me here." There was also the promise to stay in Tuskegee made to Booker T. Washington before his death in 1915. To commercial offers Carver often replied that he was a scientist, not a businessman; that his work was to build the bridges for them to cross over on.

Professor Carver was popular as a lecturer in spite of a high-pitched voice, shabby though immaculately clean clothes, and a simple style of speech. But he would go only where he believed his message was needed or would benefit the school. Everywhere he spoke he impressed his hearers with his kindliness, his sense of humor, his immense knowledge, and his sheer genius. Even prejudiced white Southerners admitted that this Negro's brain was clearly as good as any white man's! Still, though he was honored on the platform, wherever he went he had to ride in the Jim Crow car and endure all sorts of insults because of his race. He did not protest. He would not allow himself, he said, to sink so low as to hate any man.

In the First World War Professor Carver helped his country by increasing food production. He found new ways of dehydrating foods, which saved valuable ship space. He developed sweet-potato flour to substitute for scarce wheat flour. And he discovered how to make vegetable dyes to take the place of the aniline dyes formerly imported from Germany.

Honors came to him increasingly. He accepted them graciously, then went back to work. He was pleased when both Simpson College and the University of Rochester made him a Doctor of Science. Pleased, too, when he was asked to become a collaborator of the United States Bureau of Plant Industry, doing his advisory work in Tuskegee. A few friendships brought him much pleasure, especially that with Henry Ford. These two men found in each other kindred spirits; many of their methods and aims were the same. Ford called Carver "the greatest living scientist" and honored him by building at Dearborn, Michigan, a replica of his log-cabin birthplace with wood from every state. Carver in turn helped Ford in his search for synthetic rubber.

When a new modern laboratory was installed at Tuskegee, Dr. Carver chose every item in it himself. But when someone remarked, "Here you'll perform miracles," Dr. Carver replied, "Only God performs miracles. Here I'll only listen for his voice and try to carry out his instructions."

George Washington Carver's science and his religion were never at odds. His research was as if inspired; he never groped about aimlessly. Intent on great goals, he was impatient with dabblers. By nature a lone worker, it was difficult to find an acceptable assistant for him. Success came with the arrival of Austin Curtis, a young man from Cornell who was capable of carrying on his own projects and yet alert and sensitive to Dr. Carver's wishes. The two became fast friends.

In 1937, in recognition of George Washington Carver's forty years at Tuskegee, Curtis helped set up a Carver Museum. In it were nearly a thousand products the great scientist had developed from peanuts, sweet potatoes, wild vegetables and plants. Next to the exhibits of foods, textiles, medicines, and building materials was a room of Carver's flower paintings. In his honor the new science building was named Carver Hall, and at the commencement in June a bronze bust of Dr. Carver was presented to the school.

A greater tribute was reflected in the thousands of self-respecting, self-supporting students he had influenced, and in the neat painted cottages all over the Southern countryside. Flowers grew around them; chicken yards, pigpens, and vegetable plots lay between the cottages and the fields full of fluffy bolls of white cotton. The Tuskegee professor's "live-at-home, own-your-place" program had taken hold, and thousands of Negro families were enjoying better health, greater prosperity, happier lives because of it. Diversified crops, improved cotton-growing methods, and native industries had improved the economy of the whole South.

In the Second World War many of Dr. Carver's First World War recommendations were put into effect. His suggestions for food preservation and dehydration were found to be as sound in 1940 as in 1918. Many of his earlier bulletins were reissued — often, unfortunately, without credit to him or to Tuskegee.

Sensing that his years were numbered, the scientist in 1940 contributed his life savings to create the George Washington Carver Foundation for Research at Tuskegee. This would be a boon to poor boys with talent in scientific fields.

Congress honored Dr. Carver by making his Missouri birthplace a national monument as "a memorial to a humble man whose achievements . . . have been great." Road markers were set up to point the way to the birthplace of "the famous Negro scientist."

At Dr. Carver's death in 1943, tributes came from notables and from the humble. In her biography Florence Crannell Means wrote, "He gave to his people and his country uncounted millions of dollars and health and beauty and high dreams." To the world, said the president of Tuskegee, Dr. Carver gave "a method and an idea which, if ever fully grasped, will mean peace and plenty for mankind everywhere." And on the tombstone slab on the Tuskegee campus he had made beautiful were engraved the words: *A life that stood out as a gospel of self-sacrificing service. He could have added fortune to fame but caring for neither he found happiness and honor in being helpful to the world.*

I want to work for something I feel is important to man-kind.　A PEACE CORPS VOLUNTEER

A Chance to Help

The Peace Corps, Abroad and at Home *(founded 1961)*

P OVERTY in America increased as the country changed from an agricultural to an industrial society. Thousands of men and women left farms and villages to work in city factories. Thousands more came from European towns and cities to seek a better life in America. Living and working conditions in the over-crowded cities were bad. Greedy landlords and employers took advantage of the workers. Even the law seemed to favor the protection of property above the well-being of men and women.

But the poor were not without their champions. Many individuals waged war against poverty, going at it in different ways and emphasizing different wrongs. Riis fought for better housing in cities; Gompers, for better labor conditions; Julia Lathrop, to win a better chance for children and for the handicapped; Carver, to make a better life for the poor in rural areas.

By the twentieth century their battles seemed close to being won. Rapidly developing science and technology, expanding industries and trade had raised American living standards to undreamed-of levels. Yet, while American women — and men — went on reducing diets because they had eaten too much, "pockets of poverty" still existed in their own country, and more than half of the people the world round were going to bed hungry. Generous-hearted Americans sent food to the near-starving, and clothes to the near-naked, then turned back to enjoy their own plentiful prosperity.

The Second World War brought distant parts of the world much closer to America. Want, ignorance, and disease everywhere became matters of real concern to Americans. What right had they, they asked themselves, to be well fed, healthy, and comfortable while so many others barely existed? Why couldn't the scientific and technological know-how that had brought prosperity to America bring a better life to others? Why need there be abject poverty anywhere on this richly endowed globe? What could be done, above and beyond individual and small-group efforts, to make a dent in worldwide poverty and a start toward universal freedom from want?

The Marshall Plan, after the war, was the United States Government's first really big foreign-aid movement. Tightly linked to American interests, it also put war-torn Europe on its feet economically. Later, President Truman's Point Four plan — the United States Technical Assistance Program — sent trained technicians to help the peoples of peace-loving countries "through their own efforts, to produce more food, more clothing, more materials for housing, and more mechanical power to lighten their burdens." In 1954, Public Law 480, called "Food for Peace," made American surplus foods available to developing countries through sale, loan, or grant. Other Government foreign-aid programs followed. In 1961, the Agency for International Development — AID — was set up to coordinate existing programs and start other "self-help" projects. The Alliance for Progress was established to work with Latin American Governments to help fight poverty in those countries.

Private agencies, both church-sponsored and nonsectarian, stepped up their overseas programs after World War II. The Friends Service Committee, which had long been active in sponsoring summer workcamps abroad and in relieving need the world over, expanded its activities. CARE, a private organization, began to send overseas gifts from individuals and groups — food and medicine, farm tools and seeds, books and school supplies. In its close to twenty-year history CARE packages have reached thirty-five million underprivileged persons in forty countries. International Volunteer Service, Inc., has conducted service programs in nine countries. Operation Crossroads Africa has sent carefully screened student work teams to ten West African countries. And there were and are many more American group efforts to help to free people in remote lands from want.

Other nations, too, have their Government and private

agencies to wage war against poverty and help raise living standards "everywhere in the world." To share the burden more effectively among nations, the United Nations has its agencies. In its very first days UNRRA was set up to give relief and rehabilitation assistance to sufferers from the war. Later UNICEF was created to feed the thousands of starving children the world over, and UNESCO to help develop education, science, and culture on the village level. FAO was set up to give farm and agricultural help, and WHO to aid in the health field. Working separately and cooperatively, these and other UN agencies and organizations have done and are doing a wonderful job. They have put into action the responsibility the United Nations assumed for achieving a world free from want by helping the people of the world help themselves.

With all these organizations, what need was there of still another? President Kennedy, when he asked Congress early in 1961 for authority and funds to set up a Peace Corps, gave the answer. It was simply that the existing efforts were not enough. The Peace Corps, he explained, would attempt to battle poverty, develop goodwill, and build the peace in a different way. Its members would be doers rather than advisers. They would work at the grass-roots level as teachers or technicians, supplying the specific skills needed by the nation requesting their help. They would live with the people of the community served, live as they lived, and under their laws. "Our own freedom and the future of freedom around the world," the President said, "depend in a very real sense on the ability to build growing and independent nations where men can live in dignity, liberated from the bonds of hunger, ignorance, and poverty."

The difficulties a Peace Corps Volunteer would face —
privations and loneliness, fatigue and frustration, unfore-
seen hazards and dangers — were not minimized. Yet the
response was amazing; thirty-six thousand persons took the
first tests in May 1961. Young men and women, especially
on the nation's campuses, seemed to have been waiting for
just such an opportunity to be useful, for just such a chance
to help. "I want to work for something I feel is important to
mankind," more than one of them said. The low maintenance allowance did not hold them back, nor the small
salary, unpaid until the end of the service, nor the fact that
joining the Peace Corps did not cancel out military service.

Most Americans approved the President's idea, but some
clever columnists ridiculed the Peace Corps as a Boy Scout
Brigade, a Children's Crusade, or as Kennedy's Kiddy
Korps. Doubtful congressmen thought it unreasonable to
ask the Government to underwrite such an idealistic venture. Congress did agree to the President's proposal for a
"pilot project," but the Peace Corps remained very much
on trial.

It was the able administration of Sargent Shriver which
gave the Peace Corps its real start and sped it on its way.
This director, selected by President Kennedy, chose his
helpers wisely, set up policies and procedures in an un-
charted field with extraordinary skill, then carried them
through with a sort of inspired zeal.

The applicants were of all ages over eighteen, of every
creed, color, and type. They were first screened for special
skills and for personality traits such as adaptability, ingenu-
ity, humor, tact, and physical, mental, and spiritual stam-
ina. The quarter of them who came through these tests were

invited to take the vigorous training program. For from eight to twelve weeks, sixty or more hours a week, the trainees prepared for the specific assignment ahead. They were instructed in the native language and in the history and customs of the country they would go to. A basic American-background course readied them to answer questions about democracy, American style. Strenuous physical exercises put them in shape for the hard work, the long hours, and the primitive conditions to come. Four out of every five trainees finished the rigorous course and were asked to go overseas. Arrived at the field of action, the Volunteer was prepared to adjust quickly to a more primitive way of life, to work at improving his ability with the language, and to try to curb his desire to get things done in a hurry.

The first three assignments requested and carried out by the Peace Corps were the construction of feeder roads in Tanganyika, community-development projects in cooperation with CARE in Colombia, and teaching in rural districts in the Philippines. All in all, more than half the Volunteers were assigned to some sort of teaching job. Others served as nurses in hospitals, laboratory technicians, or workers in health centers, or concerned themselves with improving agricultural methods or crafts, or with the building of schools, community centers, hospitals, homes, roads, or aqueducts. Those who worked on community-development projects first gained the confidence of the local people and found what they needed most, then worked right along with them on whatever it was they decided to do.

Before the first year went by, it was clear that the Peace Corps was becoming a real force in the fight for freedom from want. Besides helping the people of other nations fill their needs for training manpower, it was giving them a better understanding of Americans. The "image" the Volunteers created was quite different from that projected by the usual overseas American businessman or tourist or diplomat. The close personal relationships which resulted from speaking the native language and living and working side by side with the people they served, made the Volunteers the finest sort of goodwill ambassadors.

The doubters began to support the Peace Corps, and the scoffers started to praise it. They talked about its spectacular achievements — how Peace Corps Volunteers had saved a rice crop from an unexpected flood, had inoculated whole villages against smallpox, had constructed roads so that isolated farmers could carry their produce to market. Less talked about but of even greater value were the Volunteers' day-after-day teaching in rural schools, their tedious tasks of bricklaying, or well-digging, or plowing and planting, or their help in the painfully slow progress of simple projects in the back country or needed enterprises in small villages. In all of them, the Peace Corps Volunteers tried to encourage the emergence of the people's skills and their will toward independent self-help. "Give a man a fish and he will eat for a day; teach him to fish and he will eat for the rest of his days," says an old Chinese proverb. The Peace Corps men and women were teaching people in many countries how to fish in a variety of ways.

"Come back and educate the rest of us," Sargent Shriver had told some of the Volunteers as they went out. After the unforgettable experience of their two-year term of service, the returning Peace Corps Volunteers could bring to stay-at-home Americans a better understanding of conditions and problems in half a hundred developing countries of the world. To whatever positions they went in public service, government, education, or business, their overseas experience enabled them to contribute a knowledge of world affairs, an ability to work harmoniously with others, and a capacity for meeting difficult situations with wisdom and skill. In many ways the Peace Corps was proving a source of strength to America.

Congress became so sold on the Peace Corps that it voted in 1963 to expand it. Director Shriver decided then not to increase the number of new Volunteers by lowering standards. Instead, he determined to require even higher standards in skills, personality traits, and language aptitudes, and a longer period of training. The overall number of Volunteers, he insisted, should be not more than fifteen thousand. His reason for this was that, more than to anything else, the Peace Corps owed its outstanding success to the high quality of the men and women in it. Historian Arnold Toynbee characterized the typical Volunteer as "Western man at his best," and so he — and she — was, and is.

The Communists' opposition to the Peace Corps is one proof of its success; so is its imitation by a dozen other countries. More important is the way it has completely changed the American concept of what is the most effective kind of foreign aid in the battle against worldwide poverty. Gone is the concept of "massive infusion of capital and sophisticated aid," and in its place is that of "limited assistance on simple but essential economic and social self-help projects," according to Pauline Madow in *The Peace*

Corps. Programs tailored to fit local needs, and skilled service to help carry them out, may well be more valuable to other countries — and to the United States — than the financing and building of huge steel plants or massive dams.

Most thinking people agree on the urgent need to wipe out world poverty quickly by compressing into decades, in many underdeveloped countries, the progress it took the Western nations centuries to achieve. In this effort, the Peace Corps's person-to-person, local-service method may, in the long run, be the fastest as well as the best plan.

The inspiring example of the Peace Corps's work abroad awakened Americans to the need for the same sort of fight against poverty in our own country. "Why couldn't the same techniques used overseas be put to work at home?" they asked. "Why need there be any "pockets of poverty" in this "richest, most productive society the world has ever known"?

Few Americans realize the extent of poverty in this land of plenty, for it is not so obvious here as in many other countries. Yet when President Kennedy appointed a committee in 1962 to study the possibility of a domestic Peace Corps its head, Robert Kennedy, reported that thirty-two million Americans — one sixth of the total population — "live in poverty and deprivation. They drift in a squalid back eddy of the twentieth century, uneducated, poorly housed, in need of medical care." In some families dependence on relief from the Government has been the way of life for three generations. Jobless, ill-trained children "inherit poverty" from jobless, ill-trained parents. Some of the poor are victims of economic change — the closing of mines or mills, automation, increased competition, shrinking markets for unskilled workers. Some are sufferers from natural disaster — floods, droughts, crop failures.

Whatever the cause, the existence of such poverty is a disgrace to the prosperous American people, especially since President Johnson has assured us that "the means are at hand to fulfill the age-old dream: poverty can now be abolished."

Half of America's poor live in rural areas. The Appalachian region, where unemployment is twice the national level, is considered to be the largest rural "poverty pocket." More than a million people have moved away because they can no longer exist in this mountainous land of abandoned mines, absentee ownership, and increasing unemployment. Others stay on, living primitively in a hand-to-mouth manner, accepting relief, and becoming constantly more hopeless, despairing, and despondent. Recently the Governors of the eleven states involved have recognized the problem, and Congress has accepted some national responsibility for its solution.

Migrant farm workers and their families represent another "pocket of poverty." Many of the children of these traveling laborers grow up knowing little but work. They exist without a real home; there is no adequate attention paid to their health; their schooling is pathetically scanty.

American Indians on reservations in many cases live under substandard conditions, with poor provisions for health and education. So do many refugees from Castro's Cuba.

In the poorer sections of cities inadequate housing and unemployment create problems. Families moving in from rural areas, thinking they will improve their condition, make bad matters worse. Children who have dropped out of school and are unable to find work roam the streets and are easily pushed along the path toward delinquency and crime.

These are some of the areas that most desperately need help, although there are others. Secretary of Labor Wirtz warned that the poor are not concentrated in a few "pockets of poverty," but that "they are everywhere in America. If they are out of sight, do not suppose they are ever more than five miles away."

No private group or groups could conquer this widespread American poverty problem. There are already too few active and in-training social workers to handle the job they are currently trying to do. Many more local volunteers could be used. But the crying need is for a centrally directed body of people with the personal qualities and abilities and useful skills required to tackle an out-and-out fight against poverty. Such a body would, to quote labor leader Walter Reuther, "take all the separate efforts and focus them in on the problem in a unified way." Its members would teach "fundamental illiterates," oversee health programs, work with disheartened men to repair or replace tumbledown homes, help rehabilitate the mentally and physically handicapped.

The domestic Peace Corps, more or less patterned after the overseas one, is even more complex than it in organization and aims. Both President Kennedy and the then Vice President Johnson believed that such a National Service Corps could play a large part in abolishing poverty in America.

President Johnson's first major legislative program, pre-

sented to Congress in 1964 and termed the Economic
Opportunity Act, asked for close to a billion dollars to open
an "unconditional war on poverty in America." Almost half
of this amount was earmarked for programs to aid young
people. The Job Corps, to be set up in close to a hundred
centers, was to train unskilled or poorly motivated youths
from sixteen to twenty-one in work habits and to carry out
special conservation projects. Other youths would do man-
ual labor and learn the rudiments of education. Local
Governments and institutions would undertake on-the-job
training, with the federal Government paying most of the
cost. Federal aid would encourage employers to hire the
"hard-core" unemployed and would assist community agencies in developing antipoverty programs locally. In rural
districts, farmers would be helped to buy stock equipment.

In 1964, the call went out for five thousand Volunteers
in Service to America — VISTA. As with the overseas
Peace Corps, they would work on a low-maintenance basis,
with no pay until the end of the term, which would be for a
year instead of the two for overseas service. Just as happened with the original Peace Corps, the applicants more
than exceeded the anticipated number. The man appointed
director of the new Office of Economic Opportunity was
Sargent Shriver, obviously the man best equipped for the
post. His initial plan involved one hundred and twenty
projects, all of them emphasizing giving people a chance to
"earn their way out of poverty."

In signing the Economic Opportunity Act, passed by
Congress after the customary debates and delays, the President stated, "It is the policy of the United States to eliminate the paradox of poverty in the midst of plenty in this

nation by opening to everyone the opportunity for education and training, the opportunity to work, and the opportunity to live in decency and dignity."

Inevitably such a tremendous program encountered questions of control of funds — whether by federal, state, or local authorities or private agencies. Yet by midsummer 1965, *Life* magazine reported that the campaign was "changing many lives for the better and spreading hope into some chronically hopeless corners." One particularly bright spot was Operation Headstart, a pre-kindergarten project aimed at preparing underprivileged children to enter school on more nearly equal terms with others.

"No federal program in peacetime has ever gone so fast," said director Shriver. And when, at the end of 1965, heading both the Peace Corps and the OEO obviously became too much, he turned over the directorship of the PC to the State Department's Jack Hood Vaughn in order to give his full time to the expanding antipoverty war.

America is now definitely embarked on a war on poverty, on a valiant battle to win freedom from want in this country as well as "everywhere in the world." And with the country committed to the effort, predicted John Galbraith, economist and author of *The Affluent Society,* "the end of poverty is inevitable."

IV

THE FOURTH IS
FREEDOM FROM FEAR

Nothing is to be feared except fear itself.   FRANCIS BACON
Nothing is so much to be feared as fear.   HENRY THOREAU
The only thing we have to fear is fear itself.

FRANKLIN ROOSEVELT

THERE ARE *many different kinds of fear. Some fears are personal, like the fear of flying, of high places, of crowds, of pain, of death. These must be conquered by individual effort. Other kinds of fear involve more than oneself and can be fought by lessening or overcoming their causes. Often this is better done by groups than by individuals. Organized efforts are reducing the fear of poverty, disease, accident, crime, flood, and destructive fire by combatting and overcoming their causes.*

One fear is universal and overwhelming — the fear of war, which involves all mankind. This is the fear singled out by Franklin Roosevelt in his Four Freedoms message. He believed that humanity could be freed from it by reducing weapons to the point where no nation would be able to go to war against another. Others suggest that war can be abolished by increasing armaments to frighten away enemy attacks; or by total disarmament; or by keeping a balance of power among the great nations; or by helping underdeveloped countries become healthful and prosperous; or by man's spiritual rebirth; or by combining strong national defense with friendly relations toward all.

Franklin Roosevelt spoke before the days of the atom bomb and the nuclear age. As more nations unlock the nuclear secret, the "blue haze of fear" persists and deepens.

Hope lies with the champions of peace as they strive, both individually and collectively, to remove the causes of war by solving urgent world problems and replacing hostility with understanding and tolerance. It is their devoted, intelligent work which may yet win freedom from mankind's greatest fear — the fear of war.

I hate war. FRANKLIN ROOSEVELT

This I know. This I believe with all my heart. If we want a free and peaceful world, if we want to make the deserts bloom and man to grow to greater dignity as a human being WE CAN DO IT! ELEANOR ROOSEVELT

Two Workers for Peace and Progress

Franklin Delano Roosevelt (1882–1945)
Anna Eleanor Roosevelt (1884–1962)

THIS STORY belongs in Part III just as much as it does here, for both Franklin and Eleanor Roosevelt worked for Freedom from Want as well as for Freedom from Fear. They saw the two as closely connected. "Freedom from fear is eternally linked with freedom from want," Franklin Roosevelt said, and both he and his wife were tireless champions of his dream of "peace and a more abundant life to the peoples of the world."

Nearly all of Franklin Roosevelt's boyhood associations were with well-established, wealthy families, and he was educated by tutors, in Europe, and at Groton — an exclusive boarding school for boys. He loved the sea and would have chosen Annapolis and the Navy, but he yielded to his father's decision for Groton, Harvard, and law school.

Eleanor was a lonely little girl who, after her parents' death, lived a dreary, dreamy life among adult relatives. She was very self-conscious because her aunts told her that she was not a pretty child. At fifteen her grandmother sent her to a girls' school in England. In her three happy years there she became more self-reliant and practical, learned much, and widened her experience by going with the school's headmistress on several trips to the Continent.

On her return, to make her debut in New York society, Eleanor again felt self-conscious and awkward. There were reasons: she did not know any of the young people at the parties she had to go to; she was dressed too childishly; she was a poor dancer; and she found it hard to make conversation. Fortunately fashionable young ladies were beginning to take up social work, and Eleanor volunteered to teach calisthenics and dancing to the children in a settlement house on the lower East Side. Here she discovered the joy of being useful and of giving pleasure to others. She joined the Consumers' League and, along with some of its members, explored a few New York sweatshops to see firsthand "how the other half lives."

Romance was not far off. Another Roosevelt — a handsome fifth cousin studying at Harvard — was so strongly attracted to this sweet, sensitive, serious-minded girl that he started coming down to New York on weekends to call. He would turn up at the dances where he thought she might be, and would drop in at her settlement-house classes to escort her home to the apartment where she was living with a young aunt. Before long Franklin and Eleanor were engaged.

Franklin's father died while he was in college, and his mother turned her devoted attention to her only child. She hoped she could keep him with her, content to lead a country-gentleman sort of life on the Roosevelt estate at Hyde Park on the Hudson. For a year she tried to dissuade him from marrying Eleanor. But Franklin intended to plan his own life. After college he entered Columbia Law School in New York, and he and Eleanor were married there on St. Patrick's Day, 1905. Theodore Roosevelt, Eleanor's uncle and then President of the United States, gave the bride away, attracting more attention at the wedding than the bride and groom.

During the summer vacation the couple had a carefree honeymoon in Europe. After their return the daily grind of law school was enlivened by an active social life, which appealed to the young husband more than his law course. He enjoyed being with people, and with his pleasant way of making himself agreeable made friends easily. After passing the state bar examinations, he became a clerk in a law firm. The contacts he made with different types of people interested him far more than the legal aspects of his work, and he soon decided that the life of a lawyer was not for him. He determined to follow "Uncle Ted" 's example and go into politics. "TR" had said that "young men of good background and education owed their country public service." Franklin knew that he was a born leader; he thought it would be exciting to use this power to bring about changes he felt were for the public good.

Eleanor accepted her husband's decision without a murmur. She was accustomed to deferring to others, especially older people, and her mother-in-law encouraged the habit. Mrs. Roosevelt, Sr., built a sort of duplex house in the city, one part for herself, the other for the young couple and their rapidly enlarging family. Six babies arrived in ten years' time; one died in infancy.

In 1910, Franklin Roosevelt ran for the state senatorship from Dutchess County, though he was a Democrat like his father before him and Dutchess County was a Republican stronghold. He spoke before many groups and drove all over the county in a flaming red Maxwell touring car decorated with flags and posters. Every time he met a horse-drawn wagon he stopped the car and turned off the engine. This consideration not to frighten the horse pleased the driver — usually a Republican farmer. It also gave Roosevelt a chance to open a conversation about the need for local reforms, clean government, and progressive measures.

Franklin Roosevelt won the New York senatorship and moved his wife and three small children to Albany. Soon he was in the limelight as the leader of a revolt against an appointee of Tammany Hall, the corrupt New York City stronghold of Democratic boss rule. His enthusiasm being greater than his political experience, Roosevelt was forced to accept a compromise appointee, but he had established himself as an opponent of Tammany Hall and a strong independent leader. In the legislature, Henry Thomas wrote, he worked for "better milk at lower prices for the children of the poor; higher wages and shorter hours for the workers; bigger profits for the farmers; free medical service for the needy; social justice for all." Two years later he was reelected. A siege of typhoid fever kept him from campaigning personally, and Louis Howe, a politically wise though physically somewhat unattractive newspaperman, ran the campaign. Howe recognized Roosevelt's political potential and continued to work closely with him in his climb to the top.

In the 1912 presidential campaign Franklin Roosevelt backed Woodrow Wilson, whose philosophy of government appealed to him strongly. After his election, Wilson made Roosevelt Assistant Secretary of the Navy. With his lifelong love of the sea and the Navy, nothing could have suited him better. He left his hardly begun second term in the New York Senate, settled his family in Washington, and happily started to "learn the ropes" of his new job. It was one which Theodore Roosevelt had held and had raised to a position of some importance several years before.

Franklin Roosevelt found it exciting to be in the midst of the national political scene. He learned fast, and he found plenty to do. The Navy was run down, its equipment was old-fashioned, and many of the personnel dated back to the sailing era. For seven years he worked to strengthen it and bring it up to date. The Navy yards, with their thousands of civilian workers, were part of his responsibility, and he learned a good deal about labor problems and relationships from them.

The last two Roosevelt boys were born in Washington in 1914 and 1916. Eleanor Roosevelt, although bored by the traditional social custom of officials' wives making calls on other officials' wives, performed the duty faithfully. More to her liking were the pleasant gatherings of congenial friends, the impromptu excursions with the children, and the rather noisy, highly informal family life at home.

Roosevelt had a premonition of the coming war and felt strongly that the United States Navy should be ready to meet any emergency. In his eagerness to prepare for anything that might come, he "danced on the edge of insubordination," testifying before congressional committees and even speaking publicly about the need to be prepared. When this country finally entered World War I, he was at his best. Encouraged now to build the Navy quickly to war strength, he slashed red tape and got things done with unbelievable speed. He wanted badly to get into uniform — in the Navy, of course — but President Wilson and Secretary Daniels considered him too valuable where he was to release him.

The war changed life for everyone, including young Mrs. Roosevelt. Like thousands of other American women she knitted sweaters and socks and did volunteer work in Government hospitals. She worked long hours in the almost unbearable heat of the Red Cross shack set up in the railroad yards to serve coffee and sandwiches to soldiers going through Washington on their way overseas. When she saw the appalling conditions in a federal hospital for mental cases she urged the Secretary of the Interior to improve them and persisted until the changes were made — changes which included the introduction of occupational therapy and the building of a recreation room. As she became more involved in affairs outside her home and social life, Eleanor Roosevelt gained confidence in her own abilities; her sense of values changed, her concern over others and her interest in national and international problems grew. After seeing maimed soldiers in hospitals she vowed that as long as she lived she would do everything within her power "so that we may have a world without war or the threat of war."

In 1916, Assistant Secretary of the Navy Roosevelt was sent overseas on an inspection tour of naval installations in the war zone and to talk with important persons in England, France, and Italy. It was a dangerous trip, and an important mission for a man in his middle thirties. He handled it well. He negotiated the dovetailing of British and American construction programs, observed details of Navy procedure, and improved Navy business techniques.

Personally, the most significant part of the trip was an excursion to the battlefront in France. Here Roosevelt saw firsthand the "tragedy and brutality" of war and lost forever any lingering notion of its glamor. The bone-weary soldiers in the muddy trenches made him feel guilty that he was not sharing their hardships and dangers. The devastated villages and farms, the burned hospitals and homes, the stench of battlefields impressed themselves indelibly on his mind and heart. Years later he wrote, "I have seen war. I have seen war on land and sea. I have seen blood running from the wounded. I have seen men coughing out their gassed lungs. I have seen two hundred limping, exhausted men come out of line — the survivors of a regiment of a thousand that went forward forty-eight hours before. I have seen children starving. I have seen the agony of mothers and wives. I hate war."

The emotional impact of this experience, added to the frenzied pace of his days and nights under difficult physical conditions, laid Roosevelt low. On the returning ship he collapsed with fever, double pneumonia, and virulent influenza, and was carried ashore on a stretcher. His wife helped nurse him back to health. During the flu epidemic she also cared for other bedridden members of the household and visited Government girl clerks desperately ill in makeshift hospitals. While convalescing, Franklin wrote a "clear-headed and able" report of his tour of duty. He still wanted to get into active service, but by the time he had recovered, the war was nearly over.

After the Armistice, Roosevelt went again to Europe, this time to supervise the disbanding of the Navy overseas installations. His wife went with him, for he was still weak from illness. Between duties they motored to the devastated war areas. "What they saw on that tour," Lorena Hickok wrote, " — the ravaged villages and farms, the filthy trenches overrun with rats, the rows and rows of little white crosses over hastily dug graves — made them both fighters for peace for the rest of their lives."

At home again, the Assistant Secretary worked as hard at cutting back naval strength as he had worked earlier to build it up. The League of Nations, so dear to Woodrow Wilson, seemed both to him and to Eleanor a logical means of achieving a warless world. It was an important issue of the 1920 presidential campaign, when Franklin ran for Vice President as running mate of James M. Cox. But in the nationalistic, isolationist reaction to the war the League lost out, and so did Cox and Roosevelt. "FDR" left Washington and went back into private life in New York, combining business and law and helping with such civic undertakings as the Boy Scouts, the Lighthouse for the Blind, and the Seamen's Institute.

With less hospital visiting to do and more time for herself, Eleanor Roosevelt began, as she said, "thinking things out for myself and becoming an individual." She had need of her new-found strength, for the next year, 1921, brought a complete overturn of life for the whole family. Joining them for a vacation period at their Campobello summer home off the Maine coast, Franklin Roosevelt was struck down by a violent attack of poliomyelitis. He endured weeks of torturing pain, along with the shock of almost complete paralysis. By painful exercises and treatments he gradually recovered the use of his hands, arms, and back, but not of his legs. For the rest of his life he must depend on braces and canes and wheelchairs. His mother urged him to retire to Hyde Park, which he loved, and lead there a quiet, easy, inactive life. His wife, and his personal and political friend Louis Howe, encouraged him to fight with every ounce of his enormous energy and will power to conquer the disability, then to disregard as far as possible whatever handicap he could not overcome. Franklin Roosevelt fought. His character was deepened by the experience, and he faced his changed life with a courage that inspired others.

At Louis Howe's suggestion, Eleanor more or less tricked her husband back into politics by becoming involved in them herself. Howe, besides having tremendous faith in Franklin Roosevelt's political future, must also have seen qualities in Eleanor Roosevelt which even she did not suspect. At his insistence, overcoming her shyness she became active in the League of Women Voters, the Women's Trade Union League, and the Women's Division of the Democratic State Committee. She brought home new friends and started political discussions which her husband could not resist joining. She talked over civic issues with him and asked his advice on the speeches she hesitantly agreed to make at women's gatherings. Her earnestness and enthusiasm, and her sincere concern for people made her a popular speaker, even though for years she was a poor one.

Mrs. Roosevelt organized her time with great care. Always her husband and children came first. She tried to take the place, to some degree, of the father in the family by learning to swim and to drive a car, and by going camping with her sons. It was a difficult period of adjustment for all the family — not the least for Mrs. Roosevelt, Sr., who had again lost out on having her son permanently with her at Hyde Park.

Both Eleanor and Franklin were much concerned with the matter of world peace. In 1923, Franklin wrote an essay for the Edward Bok competition for the best plan to achieve it. He did not submit the essay, for Eleanor was made a member of the award jury. Much later, he pointed out that its basic idea was similar to that of the United Nations.

For several years Franklin Roosevelt devoted himself to winning the full recovery he hoped for. When he found ease and comfort in the pool at Warm Springs, Georgia, he returned there repeatedly to swim in its buoyant waters. His example led other polio sufferers to the place, which he developed into a center for the treatment of the disease. Gradually he became more or less adjusted to living an active life without the support of his legs. He came back into politics strongly, running for the New York governorship in 1928, in order to strengthen Governor Al Smith's bid for the presidency.

Eleanor Roosevelt was a great help to her husband in his campaign, for by this time she had met many of New York State's political leaders. She was also busy with other things, including a furniture factory set up to give employment to out-of-work young men in the Hyde Park area and a school for girls in New York City, where she taught American history and government three days each week. When her husband won the New York governorship and the family moved into the Governor's mansion at Albany, she continued her teaching, compressing her home and hostess duties into a four-day week.

As Governor, Roosevelt expanded Al Smith's progressive program. He helped the farmers, conserved natural resources, regulated public utilities, improved state institutions, and introduced many social-welfare measures. In the summers he made extensive trips around the state to inspect prisons, hospitals, and other state institutions. While he rode around the grounds and talked to the staff, his wife inspected the interior of the buildings. She learned to see every detail and to make concise, informative reports to her husband. Increasingly she became his eyes and legs, his stand-in at wearying public functions, his informer on changing situations and attitudes. When the depression struck, she urged him to set up state-wide relief programs. She herself did everything in her power to find jobs for the jobless, food for the hungry, and shelter for the homeless.

With 1932 came the drive to put the New York Governor into the White House. Mrs. Roosevelt was happy for her husband, who looked forward to the prospect, but she disliked the idea of becoming the First Lady. She told no one how she longed just to go on "being herself" instead of being hemmed in with protocol and tradition.

Franklin Roosevelt in an unprecedented move flew to the Democratic convention to accept the nomination in person before starting a vigorous cross-country campaign. It was a bad year for the nation. The bottom had dropped out of the country's economy. People were losing their jobs, their savings, their homes and farms. Banks were closing right and left. President Hoover, though running for reelection, seemed unable to cope with the worsening situation. Roosevelt, campaigning on the theme of a bolder leadership and a "new deal" for the "forgotten man at the bottom of the economic pyramid," won by a landslide.

"This is no time for fear or timidity," he told the people in his inaugural address. "The only thing we have to fear is fear itself." He promised to put people to work, to raise the country's purchasing power, to provide adequate sound currency. His confidence brought hope to the "little man," hope sustained by the hastily enacted emergency program with its bank holiday, set interest rates, fixed prices, unemployment payment, and stock-market restrictions. The President created employment by setting up the Works Progress Administration and the Civilian Conservation Corps. He developed natural resources with projects such as the Tennessee Valley Authority. He inaugurated a fixed minimum wage and a broad social-security program. The first President to communicate with the people by radio, his persuasive "fireside chats" explained the social-reform measures which helped pull the nation out of the doldrums — and many of which became a solid part of the American way of life.

While the President was making the drastic moves to turn the tide of the Great Depression, the First Lady was using her extraordinary energy to transform the impersonal White House into a home. She arranged rooms for her husband's convenience, installed new servants' quarters, and brought equipment up to date. At Louis Howe's suggestion, she started holding press conferences for women reporters, though she refused to discuss anything political. She paid a visit to the camp of war veterans who had marched to Washington to demand immediate bonus payments, talked with them, and helped overcome their resentment toward the Government. She explored Washington slums and persuaded authorities to improve them. She began to write a weekly — later a daily — syndicated column on life in the White House, creating a personal bond with the people which brought in sacks of revealing letters.

Living in the White House, far from ending Eleanor Roosevelt's chance to "be herself," extended it immeasurably. Her interest in people and her concern for them led her to investigate conditions of out-of-work miners in West Virginia, migratory laborers in California, Dust Bowl sufferers in the Southwest, and poverty-stricken families in Puerto Rico and the Virgin Islands. Her sympathy for them made her write, speak, and use her personal influence to try to ease their lives. The intelligent reports she brought back to her husband put at his disposal her growing insight into the problems of the people of America.

In 1936, Roosevelt was elected for a second term by an avalanche of votes. Conservative objectors accused him of flouting American traditions with his experimental changes. But Roosevelt, undisturbed, declared he had only begun to fight for the third of the nation he saw "ill-housed, ill-clad, ill-nourished."

In Europe the sky was growing dark. Roosevelt tried to keep America neutral, yet not narrowly nationalistic. "We cannot and must not build walls around ourselves and hide our heads in the sand," he said; "we must go forward with all our strength to stress and strive for international peace." And he added, "We seek in every practicable way to promote peace and to discourage war."

Eleanor Roosevelt, an active member of the National Conference on the Cause and Cure of War, said, "The war idea is obsolete" — a statement for which she was severely scored. It would be easier, she suggested, "to keep out of situations which lead to war than to bring about peace once war is actually going on." Yet she saw that Nazism and fascism would have to be stopped lest they spread and destroy the freedom of men everywhere.

She stated her ideas about peace in a little book called *This Troubled World,* published in 1938. In it she advocated achieving a peaceful world through better understanding between individuals and small groups all over the world, whose ever-widening circles of influence would create a formidable world force. She urged learning the meaning of brotherly love, "making our everyday living an adventure," pointing out the horrors of war, and emphasizing the many opportunities of living heroically in peace. "We will have to want peace," she wrote, "enough to overcome our lethargy and go out and find those in other countries who want it as much as we do."

As war came ever closer to America, Eleanor Roosevelt sold defense bonds, gave money and blood, wrote and spoke — chiefly to women's groups and always donating any speaking fees to charitable causes. In addition, she was the charming, dignified, yet informal White House hostess, entertaining many important guests, including the King and Queen of England.

To build "hemisphere solidarity," Franklin Roosevelt started the "good-neighbor policy" with the Latin American countries to the south. He also sent a personal letter to the heads of fifty-four nations, asking them to enter a non-aggression pact and to cut down arms and armies, and he appealed — unsuccessfully — to Hitler and Mussolini to find a peaceful solution to their international difficulties. He persuaded Congress to forbid the shipment of implements of war to warring nations and to limit the export of war-related materials. He wanted the United States to join the World Court, but isolationist senators prevented it. "If those senators ever get to heaven," Roosevelt wrote a friend, "they will be doing a good deal of apologizing for a very long time — that is, if God is against war — and I think he is!"

Congress and the American people were opposed to anything which might lead to American involvement in European troubles. And so they "watched and worried" as Hitler took over first Austria, then Czechoslovakia. When the German armies marched against Poland, and England and France prepared to fight, Roosevelt warned the nation that war anywhere was a threat to peace everywhere, but he promised, "As long as it remains within my power to prevent, there will be no black-out of peace in the United States."

In 1940, Roosevelt faced the problem of a third term — untraditional but not illegal. He longed to retire to Hyde Park, but he did not feel he should leave the White House, for he had more confidence in himself than in anyone else to guide the nation through the "war for survival" which he saw ahead. Most of the American people shared that confidence, and they elected Franklin Roosevelt to an unprecedented third term.

A Selective Service Act was passed in the fall of 1940, and the President pledged "our national will and our national spirit and our national strength . . . to keep the peace in this New World which free men have built for free men to live in."

In January 1941 came the famous Four Freedoms speech. After pointing out in his Message to Congress the need for national defense and for helping the fighting democracies, the President went on to list the freedoms he considered essential in the postwar world. To the accepted rights of free speech and religious choice he added freedom from want and from fear. This new and sweeping concept stirred the imaginations of men and women everywhere. The Four Freedoms speech was reprinted in papers from Washington to San Francisco and from London to Shanghai. Soldiers and workers of hard-pressed Britain found in it new goals to fight and work for; Americans gained from it courage to face a darkening future.

In a radio "fireside chat" in the spring of 1941, Roosevelt again looked beyond the war and pledged, "We will accept only a world consecrated to freedom of speech and expression — freedom of every person to worship God in his own way — freedom from want — and freedom from terrorism."

That summer of 1941, Great Britain's Prime Minister Winston Churchill sailed westward through treacherous seas to a rendezvous with the United States President. On a battleship in a fogbound bay off the Newfoundland shore the two statesmen, aided by experts, planned the joint war effort, and in the Atlantic Charter stated the principles on which they "based their hopes for a better future for the world." These included the right of every people to choose their own form of government, to develop economically in a peaceful world, and to "live out their lives in freedom from fear and want."

America stood solidly behind the almost superhuman war effort which followed the Japanese sneak attack on Pearl Harbor on December 7, 1941. With Germany and Italy bound to Japan by treaty, the country was at war across the Atlantic as well as the Pacific Ocean. While directing the war effort, the President constantly kept before the people the kind of world which the war was being fought to win. The whole world, he said, was now one great neighborhood, with Americans' freedom dependent on the freedom of other peoples far away. Unless the peace assured security and freedom from fear to the whole human race, "the germs of another World War will remain as a constant threat to mankind."

The Queen of England invited Mrs. Roosevelt to come to England to see the women's war work there. This she did, visiting briefly in Buckingham Palace, then inspecting an incredible number of both British and American military camps and hospitals, Red Cross clubs and nurseries, munitions factories and bombed-out towns.

The next year, at the President's request, she journeyed to Australia, New Zealand, and dozens of South Pacific islands, traveling as an official representative of the Red

Cross. She surprised enlisted men by turning up before dawn to breakfast with them in their mess halls. She rode jolting jeeps over rough jungle trails, tramped through muddy camps in all weathers, and walked miles through countless hospital wards, pausing often to say a cheery word to the sick and wounded. All four of her own sons were in service, and there was no doubt that her heart was in her mission. Yet she admitted, "Resentment burned within me, and I wondered why we could not sit down around a table and settle our differences before an infinite number of the youth of many nations had to suffer." On that five-week trip she traveled twenty-three thousand miles, lost thirty-two pounds, and wore out innumerable escorts. Undaunted, the next year she visited soldiers stationed in the Caribbean area.

Twenty-four nations joined the United States and Great Britain on New Year's Day, 1942 — only three weeks after the United States' entry into the war — in a military alliance against Hitlerism. All of them also subscribed to the purpose and principles of the Atlantic Charter. Later twenty more nations joined the alliance, which was called the United Nations.

In September 1944, while the war still was being fought on two fronts, representatives of the United States, Great Britain, the Soviet Union, and China met at Dumbarton Oaks, an estate in Washington, to discuss the creation of an international organization to carry out the goals of the Atlantic Charter.

Eleanor Roosevelt had a greater part in its conception than many knew. Even before the United States entered the war she had recommended to her husband and some of his advisers setting up an international body "continuously to plan for future peace." She proposed that representatives of all anti-Axis countries "meet without delay to study the future structure of the world . . . to iron out differences among member nations and be prepared at the end of the war to present for final approval of the peace conference postwar policies agreed upon in principle." Her idea was rejected then as "political dynamite," but by 1944 the best minds in all the United Nations were working along these lines.

That year Roosevelt, believing it was his duty to see the war through, had taken on a fourth term, despite obvious desperate fatigue. He journeyed to Casablanca, Quebec, Teheran, and Yalta in his effort to win a permanent peace, implemented, he hoped, by the United Nations. Mrs. Roosevelt's heart ached to see her husband wearing out under the war strain. He looked haggard and ill when he sailed for Yalta where, he said, he hoped "to strengthen personal relationships with Stalin for the days of peace to come." On his return, disturbed and somewhat discouraged by Stalin's nationalistic outlook, he admitted that "peace cannot be won in a day. It can be attained only through a constant effort over a period of days upon days, years upon years." In a speech prepared soon after Yalta but never delivered, he advised, "We must cultivate the science of human relationships — the ability of all peoples, of all kinds, to live together and work together in the same world, at peace."

In the spring of 1945, at Warm Springs, where he had gone to recover his strength, Franklin Roosevelt suffered a fatal stroke. He died "a hero of the war," said Robert Taft, a political opponent, "for he literally worked himself to death in the service of the American people."

Mrs. Roosevelt went through the final ceremonies with head erect and outward calm, though her mind and heart seethed with unforgettable memories. As quickly as possible she left the White House for Hyde Park and the New York apartment she had hopefully rented before her husband's fourth-term decision. "The story is over," she told reporters at the station.

But the story was far from over. Alone and on her own, she had just two desires — to live simply and to live usefully. To accomplish the first, she turned the large Hyde Park house over to the Government, keeping for herself the cottage remodeled from the old furniture factory. To accomplish the second, she continued her daily column and other writing, her selection of girls' books for a junior book club, and her accustomed championship of worthy causes and of the underdog wherever she found him. But this was not enough.

Eleanor Roosevelt's great regret had been that her husband had not lived to see the auspicious opening of the United Nations in San Francisco, only two weeks after his death. There, with victory in sight, the representatives of the forty-six nations which belonged to the United Nations military alliance, and four more, met to establish the organization Franklin Roosevelt had dreamed of and designed and named, whose purpose would be "to maintain international peace and security." Its first working session was to be held in London in January 1946, and President Truman asked Mrs. Roosevelt to attend.

At first she hesitated, doubting her ability. Then she

accepted, for she wanted to see "Franklin's legacy to the world" started right. On the ship going over with the otherwise masculine delegation from the United States, she attended every briefing session and carefully studied notes and literature.

After a "shining" start, the London session degenerated into weary weeks of trifling, often bitter debate. Gradually Eleanor Roosevelt emerged as a strong, independent personality who restored calm to unruly meetings, parried unfair Soviet thrusts, and stood up firmly for the right of free choice. She had been assigned to the committee which dealt with the matter of refugees and of homeless children. She opposed the plan to send refugees back to their native countries against their will and finally won her point against strong Soviet oppositon. She suggested ways to solve the plight of the orphaned children and helped to create UNICEF to get food to children "who have never known what it is not to be hungry." Before returning to America she visited refugee camps on the Continent and was impressed anew with the "sickening waste and destructiveness and futility of war."

President Truman appointed Mrs. Roosevelt a member of the American delegation to the United Nations General Assembly, and she attended its meetings faithfully. She was also the United States representative on the Economic and Social Council's Human Rights Commission.

This commission was charged with writing an International Bill of Rights to define all human rights — political, civil, social, economic, and cultural. Because of their different meanings in different countries and cultures, and because of the different stages of development of various nations, this was an incredibly difficult task. Mrs. Roosevelt, elected chairman of the commission, set herself to it with seemingly tireless energy. Often she put in ten hours a day, six days a week, at headquarters and more at home. She was an ideal chairman, said Helen Gahagan Douglas, "able, courageous, persevering, always gracious, always thoughtful, even in controversy." After two years of work by the commission the Universal Declaration of Human Rights was adopted by the General Assembly in Paris in December 1948. This has been called Eleanor Roosevelt's greatest single accomplishment. Although not legally binding on the member nations until established in them by treaty or covenant, its effect was immediately felt, especially on the underdeveloped countries.

With the coming of a Republican administration in Washington the membership of the American delegation to the United Nations was changed. The respect in which Mrs. Roosevelt was held was shown by the rising ovation she received when she attended her last session of the General Assembly. "You have been a good ambassador for America," President Truman wrote her.

Working for the United Nations, which she felt represented "our one hope for a peaceful world," had become a way of life with Mrs. Roosevelt. And so she joined the staff of the American Association for the United Nations and went all over the country lecturing on the UN and organizing new state and local chapters of the AAUN.

In addition, she circled the globe — three times in five years. Everywhere she went, she talked with rulers and distinguished citizens, townsmen and villagers, college students and children. "The world," she said, "cannot be understood from a single point of view." She was careful to observe local customs. She listened and learned. She also explained and reasoned, always modestly, graciously, as a friend. She genuinely enjoyed being with people of other countries and cultures and believed implicitly in the ancient Sanskrit proverb, "Walk together, talk together, ye peoples of the earth; then, and only then, shall ye have peace."

At home, Mrs. Roosevelt went on with her speaking and her writing, her radio and TV appearances. Through every medium she urged a stronger United Nations, more consideration for the underprivileged, and — most of all — a peaceful world.

When, after eight years, another Democratic administration came into power, President Kennedy reappointed Mrs. Roosevelt to the United Nations. The delegates rose as she walked in and welcomed her with thunderous applause. Her energy still seemed boundless, her crusading spirit as strong as ever. Her family urged her to "go slow," but she did not know how. "There is such a big, muddled world," she sighed, "so much that can be done if we increase in depth of understanding." She was busily writing a book, *Tomorrow Is Now,* when overtaken by her last brief illness.

The First Lady of the World, Eleanor Roosevelt was called, and with reason. She was at home and beloved everywhere, for she lived her beliefs, and she followed her precept that "one must never, for whatever reason, turn his back on life." As her friend Adlai Stevenson so eloquently said, "She would rather light a candle than curse the darkness, and her glow has warmed the world."

The only sane policy for the world is that of abolishing war.

American Scientist-Citizen

Linus Carl Pauling (1901–   )

A SENIOR in Washington High School, Portland, Oregon, found himself in a strange situation. Because science was his great love, he had been so wrapped up in every course, every class, every activity having anything to do with the sciences that he had neglected other subjects. Now the authorities decided that his studies had been too one-sided to entitle him to his high-school diploma. And so Linus Pauling was not among the 1917 graduates at Washington High. This did not upset the young man very much, however, for he had been accepted at Oregon State College, in spite of the overbalance on the scientific side. (Forty-five years later the Portland authorities changed their minds, and Washington High School granted to the scientifically overbalanced pupil an honorary diploma—the first in its history.)

From his early boyhood, chemistry had fascinated Linus Pauling. His father, a druggist, encouraged his son to read and speculate and experiment. He saw that the boy had the talent to carry him far in the scientific world.

Naturally young Pauling studied chemistry and physics at Oregon State, majoring in chemical engineering. A book started him on an independent program of research on the electron bond. A professor recognized his ability and invited him to act as an assistant in his classes in quantitative analysis. Soon the young man was acclaimed as a scientific marvel. Long before he received his B.S. degree, he himself knew beyond doubt that his lifework lay in the field of chemical research.

The California Institute of Technology had a fine chemistry division, developed and headed by Dr. Arthur Noyes, an outstanding physical chemist. Linus Pauling journeyed down the coast to work for an advanced degree under him. At Cal Tech, too, Pauling's ability was recognized and he was made a teaching fellow. To offset his campus title of "the boy professor" he grew a luxuriant beard. He also married a beautiful girl who had been one of his star chemistry pupils at Oregon State College.

In 1925, with his Ph.D. *summa cum laude* achieved, he was able to go on to further advanced study in Europe through a grant from Cal Tech, a National Research Fellowship, and a Guggenheim Fellowship. For nearly two years Linus Pauling and his young wife lived abroad while he studied in Copenhagen, Munich, and Zurich. He worked under top scientific men, pioneering in research on crystal and molecular structure and on the new theory of quantum mechanics.

Returning to America, Linus Pauling became assistant professor, then associate professor, then full professor at the California Institute of Technology. At thirty, he had published his "Theory of Chemical Resonance" and nearly fifty other papers of original research. On receiving the American Chemical Society's award made to "young chemists of great promise," he was acclaimed as "one of the great chemists of all time."

Dr. Pauling's approach to scientific problems was unique in combining the knowledge of chemist, physicist, and biologist. Interrelating the different branches of science helped him to a better understanding of the forces which influenced the arrangement and reaction of molecules and to an explanation of some of the mysteries involved in the structure of proteins, hemoglobin, and antibodies. As a result, new drugs were developed to help control various diseases, and a gelatin substitute for blood plasma was produced. A grant from the Rockefeller Foundation provided Dr. Pauling with able assistants at the Cal Tech Gates and Crellin laboratories, of which he was now director. Following Dr. Noyes's death he also became head of the Institute's chemistry and chemical engineering divisions.

At forty, Dr. Pauling was acknowledged to be "the outstanding theoretical chemist of the United States and probably of the world." He and his staff were continually publishing important scientific papers and books. European scholars came to work under him, and he went often to Europe to attend international scientific gatherings and to lecture at universities. In the United States, too, he was in demand as a lecturer and as a visiting professor at colleges and universities. His list of awards, honorary degrees, and memberships in learned societies was long and impressive.

During World War II, Dr. Pauling put his knowledge and talents at the service of the Government. For three years he worked in the explosives division of the National Defense Research Committee, where he developed rocket explosives for the Navy, and served as a medical research consultant. Then he was appointed to the Research Board for National Security. For his wartime services he was awarded the Presidential Medal for Merit. Incidentally, he showed his independent spirit when, after Pearl Harbor, he calmly kept on as gardener a young American of Japanese descent in spite of having WE LOVE JAPS HERE signs plastered on his home.

After the war, Dr. Pauling went on with his original research into the structure of organic proteins. His aim was to understand the chemical mysteries of life and to develop ways in which to combat diseases. But his life now held another and overwhelming interest.

Like many other scientists, Linus Pauling was deeply disturbed when atomic bombs were dropped on Hiroshima and Nagasaki in 1945. The general public, he knew, had no idea of the power involved in these new bombs. Only the scientists who had helped unlock the energy of the atom realized that that act marked the beginning of a new era of world history. Far more than others, they realized that mankind must now make a choice. Men could use the newly discovered power as a war weapon, thereby running the risk of bringing to an end civilization and possibly all life on the globe, or they could abandon warfare as a means of settling disputes between nations. Dr. Albert Einstein, the world's leading scientist and the one most responsible for the discovery of the secret of the atom, said flatly, "It is no longer rational to solve international problems by resorting to war. . . . We must now make use of man's power of reason."

The year after Hiroshima, Dr. Einstein asked Dr. Pauling and seven other scientists to join with him in forming the Emergency Committee of Atomic Scientists. Since it was scientists who had unleashed atomic energy, Dr. Einstein felt it was their responsibility to warn the public that there was no possible defense against the atomic bomb and to persuade people to give up war and create a world of law and order.

Dr. Pauling took his membership in this Emergency Committee very seriously. Sincere, ardent, and idealistic, he thought that just telling people of the catastrophic effect of nuclear war would convince them that, in Einstein's words, "we must develop international law, strengthen the United Nations, and have peace in the world from now on."

But it was not that simple. The Emergency Committee, said author Robert Jungk, was "a crusade of people who were children in all political questions." The eminent scientists ran into unexpected criticism. They were even accused of being something less than patriotic because they put the survival of human beings ahead of nationalistic pride. Some of the committee members went back to their laboratories disillusioned. After five years the committee was dissolved. But Linus Pauling, feeling keenly his responsibilities as a scientist and as a citizen, went on with the crusade. He talked, he wrote, he argued against the manufacture, stockpiling, spread, and use of nuclear weapons and against all warfare as a method of solving international disputes.

In his enthusiasm for peace, Dr. Pauling supported "nearly every peace movement that came to my attention," lending his name to some organizations that may not have been entirely above reproach. Like most important scientists, he had many contacts and associations abroad and frequently traveled to Europe to lecture, attend scientific conferences, and confer with other scientists. He was vice president of the World Federation of Scientific Workers, whose president, the eminent scientist Frédéric Joliot-Curie, was a Communist. In the intensely nationalistic and anti-Communistic period which followed the war, these things were subject to misinterpretation, even by some members of Congress and the Department of State.

In 1952, Dr. Pauling was amazed and embarrassed to have his application for a passport renewal refused. He had been invited to address the Royal Society of London — an unusual honor for an American scientist — on one of his most important scientific discoveries. It was necessary for someone else to read his paper at the meeting. After two months a passport was issued, by order of the Secretary of State, which permitted Dr. Pauling to attend conferences in London and Paris. The delay, the State Department said, was because the travel was "not in the best interests of the United States." *Time* magazine, however, surmised that Dr. Pauling's anti-Communistic statements were not strong enough to satisfy the State Department, in spite of his saying under oath that he was not and never had been a Communist or Communist sympathizer. Ironically, at this very time he was under fire in the Soviet Union, where Russian scientists were being flailed for abandoning Soviet chemists' theories in favor of Dr. Pauling's theory of chemical resonance.

In his soft-spoken yet "gently resolute" way, Linus Pauling insisted on his right to speak and to associate as he saw fit. He declared he would continue to support whatever movements "seemed to me to increase the chance for a peaceful future . . . [and] to act in the way that my conscience tells me is best." When atomic scientist Dr. Robert Oppenheimer voiced objection to the H–bomb and his security clearance was withdrawn, Dr. Pauling outspokenly called the action "disgraceful." The Government, said Dr. Pauling, would have done better to have asked Robert Oppenheimer to use his great intellectual ability to help find "a practical alternative to the madness of atomic barbarism. . . . I would be proud to see the United States take the lead in bringing sanity into the world, abolishing the terrifying threat of a hydrogen-bomb war and its destruction of civilization, and initiating a future of worldwide law and order."

Dr. Pauling's passport troubles continued. The Passport Division delayed issuing him a passport to go to India, where Prime Minister Nehru had invited him to participate in the dedication of a new laboratory. Then word came that he had been awarded the 1954 Nobel Prize in Chemistry. Almost immediately the State Department provided him with an unlimited passport, including permission to visit India and Japan.

In expressing his appreciation of the Nobel Chemistry Prize, Dr. Pauling generously gave much credit to his "outstandingly able collaborators" and to the California Institute of Technology. He delivered a series of lectures at Princeton, then left for Sweden to accept the award, given especially for his research into "the nature of the chemical bond." In Stockholm he delivered a brilliant lecture on the future role of chemistry in determining the behavior of drugs in the body. Lectures, scientific meetings, and honors in the Orient followed.

Late the next year the Congressional Committee on Constitutional Rights got around to investigating Dr. Pauling's passport difficulties. Dr. Arthur Compton, Nobel laureate, testified that the State Department's restrictive passport policies were severely hampering the advance of American science by preventing free exchange of scientific information and ideas. Another Nobel laureate, Dr. Harold Urey, had earlier protested Government officials' treatment of Dr. Pauling, whom he called "a loyal and upright citizen and an extremely brilliant man."

But Dr. Pauling was more concerned about the future than the past. As both the United States and the Soviet Union increased their nuclear testing, bringing more and more radioactive fallout into the earth's atmosphere, Dr. Pauling spoke out strongly against the test explosions. He told of his concern as a scientist about the dangerous effects of radiation on the body cells of the present generation and those of the generations to come. While there could be no accurate statistics, and scientists differed as to the degree of danger, no one denied that nuclear testing did carry radiation hazards.

In June 1957, about two thousand American scientists

signed a plea prepared by Dr. Pauling urging an international agreement to stop the bomb testings. This would not only eliminate radiation damage to health but would "serve as a first step toward a more general disarmament and the ultimate effective abolition of nuclear weapons, averting the possibility of a nuclear war." The plea was presented to a subcommittee of the Joint Congressional Committee on Atomic Energy, which was just concluding hearings on the problem of radiation.

On a European lecture tour, Dr. Pauling and his wife circulated the petition, and many European scientists, including Russians, added their names. The list had grown to more than eleven thousand names from nearly fifty countries when, early in 1958, it was presented to the Secretary-General of the United Nations.

Dr. Pauling next tried a new tactic — that of filing suit against the United States Department of Defense, the Atomic Energy Commission and their Soviet counterparts to test their right to conduct the nuclear-bomb testings. Although unsuccessful, the drastic move focused attention on the perils of nuclear weapons and radioactive fallout.

About this time Dr. Pauling received the unsolicited honor of being elected to the Soviet Academy of Sciences, along with the president of the American National Academy of Sciences. Some thought Dr. Pauling should have refused this purely scientific, nonpolitical honor.

In 1957–1958, American papers gave much publicity to the controversy between two brilliant theoretical scientists — Dr. Linus Pauling, passionately dedicated to ending the nuclear-bomb tests, and Dr. Edward Teller, just as passionately dedicated to continuing them. Dr. Teller contended that the tests were necessary in order to develop the nuclear weapons on which the country's safety depended, and he pooh-poohed the idea that radioactive fallout held much risk. Dr. Pauling, stating that the stockpile of nuclear weapons was already great enough to annihilate the inhabitants of the earth twenty times over, contended that it was "not only unwise but also immoral for the people of the world to place their trust in weapons designed to kill hundreds of millions of people, to devastate the earth. The compelling need in the world today is not a need to continue the tests of nuclear weapons; it is the need to stop wasting world resources on armaments, to solve international problems by reasonable negotiations, to eliminate war, and to bring morality and justice into their proper place of prime importance in the conduct of world affairs."

In a book called *No More War!* Dr. Pauling outlined the development of nuclear weapons, presented scientific data on the harmful effects of radiation, gave the story of the ban-the-bomb petition, with its text and a breakdown of its signers by countries and by fields of science, and proposed a World Peace Organization within the United Nations for the scientific exploration of methods to achieve a peaceful world. Testing and stockpiling, he wrote, should be ended by international agreements, which should also arrange for the control of missiles and recommend steps toward disarmament.

In *No More War!* Linus Pauling states his creed concisely: "I believe that nuclear war, with its catastrophic consequences, possibly the destruction of the world, the end of civilization, must be averted. I believe that nuclear war will not be averted by a policy, followed by two great nations, of continued reliance on ever increasing force, ever greater powers of destruction. I believe that the nations of the world that are carrying out the tests of nuclear weapons are sacrificing the lives of hundreds of thousands of people now living and of hundreds of thousands of unborn children, and that this sacrifice is unnecessary. I believe that the way to avert nuclear war is to begin making safe, just, and effective international agreements; and that the first of these should include the stopping of the tests of all nuclear weapons."

And he ends his book: "We must recognize now that the power to destroy the world by the use of nuclear weapons is a power that cannot be used — we cannot accept the idea of such monstrous immorality. The time has now come for morality to take its proper place in the conduct of world affairs; the time has now come for the nations of the world to submit to the just regulation of their conduct by international law."

In the summer of 1960, Dr. Pauling was called before a Senate Internal Security subcommittee in connection with his test-ban appeal, "to see whether this sensationally successful petition effort was aided by Communist support." Dr. Pauling assured the committee that the responsibility was his alone, and willingly gave them copies of the signed petitions and of the thousand or more letters he had sent out. But he objected to disclosing the names of those who had helped collect the signatures because, he said, the role of informer was distasteful to him and he was unwilling to be a party to possible "reprisals against idealistic, high-minded workers for peace."

When the committee reconvened in the fall, Dr. Pauling was still unwilling to disclose those names. The inquiry shifted to his connection with "Communist-flavored causes." Dr. Pauling said he believed that movements dedicated to peace should be open to all, and he protested the "guilt by association" assumption. In his every statement he indicated that he was a man with courage to act independently, on the basis of his own judgment, motivated by his deep desire for world peace. The subcommittee turned up nothing to indicate any Communist influence, nor did it order Dr. Pauling to produce the list of petition circulators. If it had done this, his refusal would have led to a contempt of Congress charge. But the committee's authority seemed uncertain, and the guarantees of the Constitution's First Amendment more than sufficient to uphold Dr. Pauling's refusal.

Dr. Pauling's scientific achievements continued to go on apace. He produced a theory for understanding mental deficiencies on a chemical basis, an improved anesthetic, and a synthetic insulin. Yet in spite of his great love of, and genius for, science, he gave up some of his responsibilities at the California Institute of Technology in order to find added time to crusade for peace. He was an effective lecturer. Although he perhaps may have oversimplified somewhat, his manner and his words were so convincing — as well as lively and even humorous — that he influenced many, especially young people, and set them to working for disarmament and peace. Even those who held back, finding Dr. Pauling's solutions to world problems "unrealistic" and "utopian," admired this slender, smiling, wispy-haired, blue-eyed, gentle-seeming man for his forthrightness and his fighting qualities.

For several years Dr. and Mrs. Pauling met occasionally with disarmament enthusiasts from other countries to discuss ways of promoting world peace. On scientific journeys to Europe and to Asia, the Paulings kept in touch with the crusaders for peace in other lands. In Oslo they called a meeting of scientists and other scholars from fifteen countries just ahead of a NATO conference convened to consider the use of atomic weapons. The scholars worked out an appeal for a treaty to halt the spread of nuclear weapons; they also pleaded for a swift conclusion of the long-delayed treaty to ban atomic tests. In London and even in Moscow Dr. Pauling boldly criticized the Russians for contaminating the atmosphere with their atomic tests, and praised the United States for its decision to conduct further atomic testing underground.

In the 1960's, Dr. Pauling did not brush aside personal criticism as lightly as he once had done. He complained of articles about him in various magazines and newspapers, even suing some of them for questioning his sincerity or his patriotism. Yet he did not lose his sense of humor. One afternoon, before changing his clothes to attend a dinner for Nobel laureates at the White House, he picketed before its gates with a band of test-ban advocates, carrying a sign that read, WE HAVE NO RIGHT TO TEST!

At a ceremony honoring him as the 1961 Humanist of the Year, Dr. Pauling spoke optimistically of mankind's advances in minimizing suffering and its increasing ability to meet world problems sanely and morally. He proposed steps to speed the move toward peace but warned that "all international agreements must be made with great care," and disarmament measures "always with the best possible system of controls and inspection."

A man deeply appreciative of the beauties of the world about him, Linus Pauling loved the rugged California mountains and enjoyed climbing their hazardous trails. In the fall of 1963, he went with his wife to a cabin far from telephones and other distractions of civilization, to relax and to read proof on a chemistry text. He was overjoyed that a partial nuclear-weapon test ban — the goal for which he had been crusading for years — was to go into effect on October 10.

On that very day a forest ranger appeared at the Pauling cabin asking him to come to the ranger station to receive a telephone message. It was the notification from Norway that Linus Pauling had won the deferred 1962 Nobel Peace Prize.

Dr. Pauling could hardly believe it. It was a wonderful day, he said, for this announcement to be made. He hoped the award would help to "make it respectable" to work for peace! Later that day, when told that he was the first man ever to receive two Nobel awards, he was asked which of the two — the Prize in Chemistry or the Peace Prize — he considered more important. Without hesitation, Dr. Pauling answered, "Today's, because I feel so strongly about the need for peace and an end to human suffering from wars."

Not everyone rejoiced that the Nobel Peace Prize had come to Linus Pauling. His outspoken opposition to nuclear-weapon testing and his persistent pursuit of peace had aroused much antagonism in the American press. He was called many unpleasant names, from a "placarding peacenik" and a "dangerous nuisance" to a scientist who "doesn't know enough to stay in his own field." But the press also pointed out that he had been "as quick to condemn Soviet tests as tests held by his own country," and that he had done a service in publicizing the "dangers he estimates fallout does to human beings." One city paper even commented philosophically, "Nonconformists often play a lonely role in our society, but society for its own health needs them."

At the award ceremony in Oslo, Norway, on December 10, 1963, Gunnar Jahn, chairman of the Nobel Peace Prize committee, acclaimed Dr. Pauling for his long campaign against the testing, spread, and use of nuclear weapons and "against all warfare as a means of solving international conflicts." He went on to say, "No one would suggest that the nuclear test ban is the sole work of Linus Pauling. But does anyone believe that the treaty would have been reached if there had been no responsible scientist who tirelessly, unflinchingly, year in and year out, impressed on the authorities and on the general public the real menace of nuclear tests?"

The next day the *New York Times* quoted these words in an editorial, adding, "That scientist was Dr. Pauling. His courage in running against the crowd is now being recognized."

In Dr. Pauling's Nobel Lecture, which he called "Science and Peace," he credited the discoveries of scientists with forcing the world to move into "a period of peace and reason." He urged United Nations supervision of nuclear stockpiles, and expressed the belief that "the great goal of a world without war is in sight."

The *Bulletin of the Atomic Scientists* saw in this honor to

Dr. Pauling the recognition that "in our time scientists have become an important influence in man's struggle." Commending the Peace Prize winner for "his relentless and dedicated campaign" against nuclear-weapon testing, it saluted him as a "scientist-citizen" of courage, energy, and integrity.

Soon after learning of his award, Dr. Pauling left the California Institute of Technology to join the staff of the Center for the Study of Democratic Institutions, at Santa Barbara, California. In this organization, concerned with "the impact of science, technology, and war on democratic societies," Dr. Pauling felt he would be better able to work for peace and nuclear disarmament. As Research Professor of Physical and Biological Sciences, he would go on with his independent research in experimental medicine, but his primary concerns would now be peace and world affairs.

All through 1964 and 1965, Dr. Pauling continued both his scientific research and his work for peace. In New York he offered a program for the "national-international" control of nuclear weapons. In Berlin he criticized the idea of a multination nuclear NATO fleet. In Paris, speaking at UNESCO House on the role of science in today's world, he said, "It is the special duty of the scientist, with his special knowledge and understanding . . . to help his fellow citizens to reach the right decisions." With seven other Nobel Peace Prize winners he signed an appeal to world leaders to negotiate a settlement in Vietnam.

Linus Pauling's declarations have always been both forthright and optimistic. "No dispute between nations can justify nuclear war." . . . "It is the duty of everyone to work in whatever way he can to achieve a world from which war has been abolished." . . . "In working to abolish war from the world we are working also for human freedom, for the rights of individual human happiness." . . . "We shall utilize the resources of the world and the discoveries of science for the benefit of human beings all over the world . . . and [shall develop] a culture worthy of man's intelligence."

Nonviolence . . . may become the answer to the most desperate need of all humanity.

Nonviolent Civil-Rights Leader

Martin Luther King, Jr. *(1929–   )*

THE YOUNG theological student leaned forward in his seat, not wanting to miss a word. The lecturer, recently returned from India, was talking about Mahatma Gandhi, the great Indian leader who, by the force of his nonviolent resistance, started a social revolution and changed the history of a whole country. Here at last was the philosophy this young student—Martin Luther King, Jr.—was seeking. All the way back from Philadelphia's Fellowship Hall to Crozer Theological

Seminary, a few miles out of the city, he sat as in a daze, pondering on what he had heard and on the power of Gandhi's philosophy.

In the Crozer library young King read more — and more, and more — about Gandhi and his ideas on nonresistant direct action. Then he read all he could find about America's Henry Thoreau, who had inspired Gandhi with his ideas of moral law and of civil disobedience. Since early childhood, as the son of a Baptist clergyman, King had been steeped in the teachings of the Sermon on the Mount. Now the ideas of Jesus, Thoreau, and Gandhi all seemed to fuse into a single philosophy of social action which fitted perfectly with his own natural feeling.

Martin Luther King had always preferred to talk himself out of situations where others might have used force. As a small boy he would never hit back when pommeled by his younger brother or fight when attacked by the school bully. It was not that he lacked courage; it was just that he had no taste for violence.

Martin's childhood in the city of Atlanta, Georgia, was an essentially happy one, with a strong, rather domineering father, a gentle, understanding mother, and an older sister and younger brother. White people were not very important in his life, for most of his friends and associates were Negroes like himself. Yet he had his share of unpleasant experiences because of racial discrimination. More than once the white driver of a bus had ordered him to get up and give his seat to a white person — and had called him names if he did not move fast enough. The first time he ate on a train, behind screens drawn between him and the section for white people, he had felt, he said, "as if a curtain had come down across my whole life." He resented the "white supremacy" of the South, but life was too full of interesting things for him to worry much about it.

Because of his keen mind, Martin was ready for college at fifteen. He entered Morehouse, Atlanta's Negro college and his father's alma mater. He rather thought he wanted to be a doctor or a lawyer, though his father hoped he would become a minister. Continuing to live at home, he sang in the college glee club, was popular socially, and an active member of the Atlanta interracial intercollegiate council. He was also among the top students in his class. Summers he worked, usually in Atlanta, but once in the Connecticut tobacco fields. In his senior year he chose the ministry over law or medicine and enrolled in the Crozer Theological Seminary in Chester, Pennsylvania, to prepare for it. At his graduation from Morehouse, he was considered a bright young man "who seems to know where he wants to go and how to get there."

At Crozer, where he was one of six Negroes among a hundred or so students, Martin was elected president of the student body. Besides his theological studies at the seminary, he took sociology and philosophy courses at the University of Pennsylvania. His concern over the racial problem and his sense of social responsibility began to deepen. Gandhi's philosophy of nonviolent resistance intrigued him, though in an intellectual rather than a practical way.

Martin Luther King was valedictorian of his graduating class at Crozer, and was granted a twelve-hundred-dollar fellowship for two years of study at a graduate school. His father's parishioners, who had made him an associate pastor

of their church, urged him to return to Atlanta, but he was
eager to go on with his studies, and his father encouraged
him to do this. He decided on Boston University, and drove
north happily in a small green car his parents had given him
as a graduation present. Besides studying for his Ph.D. at
Boston University, he took several philosophy courses at
Harvard. He also found time to meet and fall in love with
Coretta Scott, a voice student at the New England Conserv-
atory of Music. She had come there after graduating from
Antioch College in Ohio; her home was in Alabama. After
several months' courtship Coretta and Martin were married
in June 1953.

Then came a year together in Boston while Coretta
completed her three-year music course and Martin his graduate work at B.U. By August 1954, his residence require-
ments were fulfilled, though he still had his thesis to write.
He was offered several pastorates and college professor-
ships, both in the North and in the South. He and Coretta
decided on a church in Montgomery, Alabama. "I wanted
to turn my talents to our Negro cause down here, to do my
part in this tense period of transition," he said.

In spite of his youth and his even more youthful appearance, he soon was recognized as a sympathetic pastor and a
thoughtful, impressive preacher. During that first year as
pastor of a Montgomery Baptist church, he wrote his
doctor's dissertation, receiving his Ph.D. in June 1955. The
Kings were settling down happily in Montgomery, antici-
pating a long, helpful ministry, when suddenly, toward the
end of 1955, a crisis hit the Alabama state capital "like the
bursting of a huge dam." Overnight the Montgomery Negroes' bitter resentment at being treated as inferiors rose

like rushing water, threatening the peace of the city with its unpredictable force.

It started when a weary Negro woman was hauled off to jail for refusing to get up and give her bus seat to a white man. Every Negro sympathized with her, remembering the insults and belittlings he himself had suffered over the years. A group of them — no one ever knew just who they were — wrote and circulated a mimeographed sheet urging all Negroes to stay off the buses until this sort of thing was stopped. The response was amazing; ninety-five per cent of the Montgomery Negroes stopped riding the buses. Since two thirds of the bus passengers were Negroes, this was a telling blow. White people thought the bus boycott would not last, but the Negroes' feeling was so strong that they were willing to walk to work — miles and forever if necessary — rather than to submit any longer to the demeaning, abusive Jim Crow treatment.

The ministers and other Negro community leaders met together to guide the spontaneous uprising into peaceful, effective channels. They formed the Montgomery Improvement Association, with the slogan "Justice without violence," and elected as its president the forceful new minister, Martin Luther King. They also organized a voluntary car pool to help get the walking Negroes to their jobs. Within a few days this was running smoothly, while the buses remained practically empty.

In accepting the leadership of the boycott, young Dr. King had not the remotest idea of what he was getting into. He was just trying to do his part in a movement with which he was in sympathy. His first step, that of attempting to negotiate with the bus company, came to nothing. But the holding of almost nightly protest meetings in different churches was a great success. It welded the Negroes — rich and poor, educated and uneducated — into an effective unit, pledged to work against racial injustice in Montgomery.

One evening, while he was speaking at one of these mass meetings, Dr. King's house was bombed. Luckily his wife, their baby, and a visiting woman friend were not in the front room, which was demolished. An angry crowd of Negroes gathered on the lawn before the house. City officials ordered them to disperse, but they would not stir until Dr. King arrived and assured them that no one was hurt. When he asked them to put away any weapons and go quietly home, they did so — to the great relief of the white officials.

The men who bombed Dr. King's house were never tried, but Dr. King was. He and other leaders of the Montgomery Improvement Association were charged with "hindering a lawful business without just cause." Able Negro lawyers defended them, showing that the Negroes did indeed have just cause for boycotting the buses. One Negro after another told of the abuses and insults he had suffered from bus drivers over the years. In spite of this, the court found Dr. King guilty and fined him.

"We're not going to ride the buses now for sure!" the Negroes declared. Thoroughly aroused, they began to realize that they had started something big. They flocked to the evening meetings to sing inspiring songs and to listen to their leaders. At every meeting Dr. King talked about keeping the boycott peaceable, about never using violence, no matter how tempted, for "ours is the weapon of love."

His intellectual understanding of Gandhi's and Thoreau's methods was being put to a practical test. He explained that there was nothing cowardly about nonviolent resistance, that it took a strong man to stand up for his rights and not hit back. People, he said, risked their bodies, even their lives, in this spiritual method of attacking evil, of seeking justice and the end of oppression without hatred or hurt. The bus boycotters listened and heeded as he urged them to respect themselves, forget their fears, "walk straight," and "overcome evil with good."

The demands of the Negroes rose as the whites' resistance stiffened. From mere respectful treatment in the buses they reached out for first-class citizenship, equal rights, more job opportunities. The movement spread from Montgomery to other cities and towns in the Deep South. The Southern Christian Leadership Conference was formed, with Martin Luther King as president and with member organizations in many communities.

The bus boycott came to an unexpected and successful end after nearly a year of protest when the Supreme Court ruled unconstitutional Alabama's state and local laws requiring bus segregation. Joyfully the Negroes went back to riding the now desegregated buses. Dr. King urged his people not to brag about the victory but to act with dignity and "in such a way as to make possible a coming together of white people and colored people on the basis of real harmony of interests and understanding."

Martin Luther King, Jr., was now accepted as the foremost leader of the Negro struggle for equal rights. He was invited to speak in many places and to write articles for magazines with nationwide circulation. He accepted his deep involvement humbly and gave himself to it completely. He knew he faced dangers daily from hate-filled persons who could not tolerate change, but his strong spiritual beliefs "cast out fear." It was "the quality, not the longevity, of life" that was important, he said. A deeply moving speaker, "combining intellect with intensity," he inspired his listeners to courage and determined resistance to injustice. Medals and honorary degrees came to him for embodying "the spirit of the new Negro"; and for leading the people "with quiet dignity, Christian grace, and determined purpose."

Dr. King worked so ceaselessly in his effort to deepen and extend the nonviolent movement that he grew physically weary. As a sort of working holiday, he and his wife went on vacation to Africa at the time Ghana was becoming an independent nation. Dr. King was greatly moved by the occasion. "The march of freedom is backed up by so many forces that it ultimately cannot be defeated," he declared, and he said that he looked forward to the creation of "a big brotherhood on earth."

A later visit to India, the land of Gandhi, was something of an emotional pilgrimage. Here Dr. King paid tribute to the memory of the courageous man whose ideas had inspired him years before and now underlay the whole nonviolent resistance movement he was leading in America.

Stronger federal laws were badly needed to bring long-denied rights to Southern Negroes. To give impetus to civil-rights legislation, Negro leaders held a Prayer Pilgrimage for Freedom in the nation's capital in May 1957, and Dr. King and others spoke before thousands in front of the Lincoln Memorial. Many Negroes were disappointed in the watered-down civil-rights bill which was finally passed, but Dr. King and Roy Wilkins, head of the National Association for the Advancement of Colored People, agreed that it was better than nothing, and promised that they would soon be back for more.

As the nonviolent protest movement gained momentum, Dr. King was described as the "man on the go." He made over two hundred speeches in 1958, all over the country, in addition to his administrative work and his preaching. Yet somehow he found time to put into a book, *Stride Toward Freedom,* the exciting story of the Montgomery bus boycott.

As Dr. King was autographing copies of his book in a store in the Harlem section of New York, a deranged Negro woman stabbed him with a steel letter opener. Dr. King sat calmly rigid, with the deadly instrument sticking out from his chest, while he was moved in his chair to an ambulance and on to a hospital. After a delicate operation, the surgeon said that the victim had been "within a sneeze" of death; any sudden movement would have forced the sharp point into the heart. For a few days Dr. King had time to meditate on his statement that the road to justice and equality was not a safe or easy one.

In Alabama, opposition grew to what some termed the King crusade to "destroy the Southern way of life." There were threats, abuses, jailings, and bombings, but with every outrage the spirit of the Negro protesters soared, and their will to resist, nonviolently. The movement spread to Negro college campuses, where the young people caught the fever and began to organize their own "sit-ins," marches, and "freedom rides." Dr. King often acted as adviser and in many cases as a leader and participant in these efforts to desegregate public places, lunch counters, and buses. It was a difficult, never-ending task to hold the fearless enthusiasm of these militant young people within bounds, to convince them of the power of love and the wisdom of nonviolent methods. Classes were set up to train leaders in the meaning, techniques, and effectiveness of nonviolent resistance.

Early in 1960 Dr. King gave up his Montgomery church and moved to Atlanta, headquarters of the Southern Christian Leadership Conference. Besides being its president, he also became co-pastor of his father's church. With his many duties, and as the "traveling salesman of Negro rights," he had few quiet days. He was arrested for taking part in a department-store sit-in in Atlanta while on probation for driving in Georgia with an Alabama license. He was handcuffed and taken to the state prison. Authorities soon released him, realizing that he would be too effective as a martyr behind prison walls.

This struggle in America, Dr. King kept pointing out, was part of a worldwide movement for freedom and human dignity. "How we deal with this crucial problem of racial discrimination will determine our moral health as individuals, our political health as a nation, our prestige as a leader of the free world." And he warned, "It isn't going to be easy. But it is the critical struggle of our time."

During the early 1960's, Dr. King urged Government leaders to pass meaningful laws and to see that existing ones were enforced. He tried to prod Negroes into registering to vote, in spite of terrorism and other obstacles, in order to put in office more men who "stand forthrightly for human rights." He attempted to awaken the "sleeping conscience of the moderate whites" and to stir them into action.

From one end of the land to the other, Dr. King carried his message. He warned that improvement was too slow and too slight for the Negro who had waited so long and who now had "a new sense of dignity and of destiny." Doing only a little — "tokenism" — was like a "tranquilizer that removes the stress just for the moment." He urged advancing boldly into the new world made by industrialization, technology, and economic changes, breaking down barriers, especially those of inequality. People should not expect to enjoy the benefits of the present while continuing to live in the past.

And then came Birmingham. There, in the spring of 1963, the Negroes dramatized their demands with marches and sit-ins. The demands were for a biracial council, for fair hiring practices, and for desegregated lunch counters.

In his book *Why We Can't Wait,* Martin Luther King told the story of Birmingham, where the Negroes' outcry for equality was met "with bombs and snarling dogs, shots in the night, death in the streets and churches, lashing fire hoses." Wave after wave of Negroes advanced, refusing to be intimidated by police dogs, clubs, and fire hoses. As they were hauled off to jail they shouted, prayed, and sang their rallying song, "We Shall Overcome." The shocking brutality of the Birmingham police force turned the eyes of the world on this "citadel of blind, die-hard segregation" and brought moral and financial support from all over the globe.

During the Birmingham campaign, over three thousand Negroes were jailed, including Dr. King. His "Letter from Birmingham Jail," published in the *Atlantic* and as a chapter of *Why We Can't Wait,* has been termed a minor modern classic. It presents Dr. King's basic philosophy, answers specific criticisms, and expresses his disappointment at the lack of support received from white moderates and from the leadership of the white church. It overflows with courage, faith, goodwill, and brotherhood.

Birmingham city officials, impressed with the determination and the nonviolence of the Negroes, agreed to negotiations, which at last brought a peace pact. At this, white segregationist extremists, "consumed with fury," bombed Negro homes and churches, beat up innocent Negroes, and tried to incite riots. Reactions came fast. The federal Government stepped in to prevent the "sabotage of a fair and just pact." The state supreme court ruled the brutal police commissioners out of office. Even more important, in Washington the shelved civil-rights bill was dusted off and put at the top of the congressional calendar.

A remarkable event climaxed the summer of this hundredth year after Lincoln's signing of the Emancipation Proclamation. More than two hundred thousand Negro and white citizens from all over the nation joined in a peaceful March on Washington. They carried banners urging the speeding up of school integration, of desegregation in the South, of job opportunities for Negroes. Together they sang freedom songs and listened to Negro spokesmen. They heard Dr. King, at his dramatic best, tell the great multitude of his dream for a better America, for a country of compassion and concern, where men would be judged not by color but by character.

Impressive though it was, the March on Washington did not solve the problem of unemployment among Negroes — far greater than among white persons — nor the problems of Negro housing, education, and legal difficulties. Nor did it satisfy impatient, aroused young Negroes who wanted to use more forceful methods than Dr. King's to fight conditions they found intolerable. *Time,* in its feature article when honoring Dr. King as its 1963 Man of the Year, said he worked twenty hours a day trying to "turn the potential for violence into successful, direct nonviolent action."

The 1964 passage of a strong national civil-rights bill was a great stride ahead, but there was still, as Dr. King kept repeating, "a long, long way to go." Demonstrations, he felt, were a means not only of keeping the issues alive but also of giving the Negroes "a chance for letting a lot of bitterness out in a creative way." And so demonstrations in Alabama and other Southern states grew in volume. The Negro's determination and his "sense of destiny" were bolstered by the "rolling tide of world opinion" and the emergence of colored nations in Africa.

International recognition came to the civil-rights cause when Martin Luther King, Jr., was awarded the 1964 Nobel Peace Prize "for the furtherance of brotherhood among men." This high honor was, he said, a tribute "to all gallant Negroes and white persons who have followed a nonviolent course in seeking to establish a reign of justice and a rule of love across this nation of ours."

At thirty-five, Dr. King was the youngest man ever to receive the award, and the third Negro; the others were America's Dr. Ralph Bunche and South Africa's Chief Albert Luthuli. Dr. King went to Oslo, Norway, for the ceremony. On his way, he preached to an overflow audience in St. Paul's Cathedral, London, on the use of nonviolence in the worldwide struggle for justice and freedom.

At the colorful Oslo ceremony the chairman of the Nobel Peace Prize committee hailed Dr. King as an undaunted champion of peace and called him "the first person in the Western world to have shown us that a struggle against race discrimination can be waged without violence." Dr. King, in accepting the award "on behalf of the civil-rights movement and all men who love peace and brotherhood," spoke of nonviolence as "the answer to the crucial political and moral questions of our time."

In an hour-long address the day after the award ceremony, Dr. King told Oslo University students and others that nations would do well to experiment with the philosophy and strategy of nonviolence. Political agreements, he said, are no longer enough to safeguard life in a world armed with weapons that can annihilate humanity. Nor is it enough merely to say that we must not wage war; we must seek and discover a way to live together in peace. "Nonviolence, the answer to the Negroes' need, may become the answer to the most desperate need of all humanity."

Almost without exception, individuals, organizations, and the press both in Europe and in America applauded the Peace Prize choice. They credited Dr. King's moderating influence with forestalling what could have become a violent and bloody period in America's social revolution. And they pointed out that nonviolence was conducive to international as well as to domestic peace.

Back in the United States, Dr. King was honored in New York, in Washington, and in his home city of Atlanta, Georgia. Of all his honors, this last was probably the one which gave him the greatest personal satisfaction. It moved him deeply to hear the mayor of Atlanta call him a man destined to help shape the future course of the world, and one willing to turn the other cheek as he pursued his quest for full citizenship for all Americans. Dr. King accepted the tribute in a voice husky with emotion, and declared that he would "neither equivocate nor compromise" in the struggle to achieve racial equality. Already he had announced that he would put every cent of the fifty-four thousand dollars which went with the Nobel Prize into the civil-rights movement.

Leaving the honor-receiving mountaintop for the valley of abuse and danger, Dr. King returned to the segregationist stronghold of Selma, Alabama, to continue his campaign of "creative and nonviolent plaguing" in the effort to win first-class citizenship for the American Negro. In March 1965, he led a historic four-day march from Selma to Montgomery, the state capital, to call to people's attention the denial of Negroes' voting-registration rights. After this he turned his attention to the cities of the North, seeking to improve housing and job opportunities for Negroes and to lead them into the mainstream of American life.

Receiving the Nobel Peace Prize, Dr. King feels, commits him to a greater involvement in international affairs and a greater effort to help solve, nonviolently, the worldwide problems of racial injustice, poverty, and war. His goal, like Franklin Roosevelt's, is "a country and a world where men and women of all races, colors, and creeds can live, work, speak, and worship in peace, freedom, and security."

Uniting for Peace

The United Nations (founded 1945)

FRANKLIN D. ROOSEVELT, when he was Assistant Secretary of the Navy, attended some of the Paris Peace Conference sessions which followed the First World War and returned to New York on the same ship as President Woodrow Wilson. The President's ideas for a League of Nations to keep the peace impressed young Mr. Roosevelt. He campaigned for the League and shared President Wilson's deep disappointment when the Senate rejected the idea of United States' membership in an international organization.

From its headquarters in Geneva, Switzerland, the League of Nations accomplished many important things during the twenty-five years of its existence. But it failed in its major purpose of maintaining peace, partly because it was not strongly enough organized and partly because it lacked the support of the United States.

During the Second World War, when Franklin Roosevelt himself was President, he felt that only the joint effort of the peace-loving nations of the world could prevent another great war. He believed that by careful planning and a strong charter, and with the United States as an active member, a world organization pledged to work for peace could succeed where the League had failed.

When Roosevelt met Churchill off the coast of Newfoundland in August 1941, the two statesmen, besides planning cooperative measures in the war effort, looked beyond the war years. In their joint statement, the Atlantic Charter, they defined the principles on which they based their hopes "for a better future for the world."

Less than four months later, the Pearl Harbor tragedy plunged the United States into the war on two fronts. Within the month, on New Year's Day, 1942, representatives of forty-four nations pledged full military and economic support to the defeat of the Axis powers — Germany, Italy, and Japan — and subscribed to the "purposes and principles" of the Atlantic Charter.

While the war still raged, delegates from these United Nations met at Hot Springs, Virginia, to consider the postwar problem of food for the starving people in war-devastated countries. They arranged to set up an office in Washington for the exchange of information about crops, food shortages and needs in their various countries. In order to feed the hungry mouths that could not wait for the long-range food and farming programs they had in mind, they organized the United Nations Relief and Rehabilitation Administration (UNRRA) to act more quickly to feed the starving.

The Soviet Union, then an ally fighting heroically against Germany, pledged its support to the joint effort for world security and peace in the Moscow Pact, in November 1943. This was also signed by China, the United Kingdom, and the United States. Its Article Four recognized "the necessity of establishing at the earliest practicable date a general international organization, based on the principle of the sovereign equality of all peace-loving states, and open to membership by all such states, large and small, for the maintenance of international peace and security."

Delegates from these same four countries met a year later at Dumbarton Oaks, in Washington, to plan for the international organization. Their detailed "Proposals" were sent to the militarily allied nations for study. Representatives of these nations already had met at Bretton Woods, New Hampshire, to consider the financial problems which would face the postwar world and had worked out the plan for a World Bank and an International Monetary Fund. The foundations of the United Nations were laid down at these meetings.

Roosevelt, Churchill, and Stalin, meeting at Yalta in February 1945, set the date and place for the conference to establish the world organization. The date — April 25, 1945; the place — San Francisco, California. Invitations went out to all the wartime allies and to a few additional countries.

On the appointed day, men and women converged on the West Coast city from all quarters of the globe. In addition to the delegates of the participating nations there were aides, experts in special fields, reporters and commentators, and interested onlookers. It was a colorful, significant occasion. One unhappy note was the absence of Franklin Delano Roosevelt, who had died only two weeks earlier.

The task before the gathering was the tremendous one of creating a new world organization that would keep the peace and promote human welfare. Could they, with care, intelligence, and dedication, avoid the mistakes of the old League of Nations? They would try!

Each of the nations represented had studied the Proposals worked out at Dumbarton Oaks, and many had changes to suggest or new ideas to add. Large or small, every nation had an opportunity to make its voice heard. In two months of hard work the San Francisco Conference turned the United Nations military alliance into an international organization for peacetime and approved and signed its lengthy Charter.

The United Nations is organized around six main divisions. First comes the General Assembly, which is a sort of "town meeting of the world," a forum for the discussion of any subject of international importance. Each nation is permitted five representatives but only one vote. The General Assembly meets annually, presided over by a chairman elected from a different nation each year. Its duties include managing the affairs of the organization, electing the members of the other divisions, and voting in new member nations.

The second division, the Security Council, has the special responsibility of keeping the peace. This division had only eleven members; in 1965 a Charter amendment increased the number to fifteen. Five of them — the United States, the United Kingdom, the Union of Soviet Socialist Republics, Nationalist China, and France — are permanent members, and the others are elected biannually from the other UN member nations, with an eye to geographical distribution. The Security Council is in continuous session, so that complaints about international situations which threaten the peace can come before it at any time. After reading reports, hearing witnesses, and perhaps sending out a commission to gather more information, the matter is discussed and peaceful solutions are suggested. If these do not work, the Council may vote to apply economic sanctions — cut off supplies and credit to choke off the war. Or it may vote to consult with the military staff which is attached to this division and consider using military units supplied by United Nations members. This is a power the old League of Nations did not possess. It has been used by the UN on several occasions — in Korea, Egypt, the Congo, and on Cyprus.

A troublesome detail in the organization of the Security Council is the veto. Because the San Francisco Conference believed that the great powers should be in full agreement on any matter involving war, each permanent member was given the right to veto any Security Council vote. It was thought that this right would hardly ever be used, but the Soviet Union has made a habit of vetoing practically every measure suggested by the Western powers. This stumbling block to action can be overcome, however, by transferring the matter to the General Assembly on a vote of nine

Security Council members. Because of the veto situation, the Security Council has lost in importance, and the General Assembly has gained.

The third division of the United Nations is the Economic and Social Council. Long made up of representatives from eighteen nations, in 1965 the number was increased to twenty-seven. Its concern is with nonpolitical matters such as health, education, and human rights. The founders of the United Nations recognized that these not only contribute to the well-being of the world's people but are important in maintaining peace, since most wars are caused by economic or social troubles. This division supervises several commissions and fourteen specialized agencies, each of which deals with some particular phase of human welfare.

The Trusteeship Council was more important when the United Nations was organized than it is today, because so many of the countries which were territories or colonies then have since become self-governing nations. Many of them are now members of the United Nations. To get a balanced viewpoint, half of the members of the Trusteeship Council are nations which control trust territories; the other half do not. Regular reports are made on conditions in the few remaining trust territories, most of which are small areas in Africa or among the Pacific islands.

The International Court of Justice, although set up anew by the United Nations, is really a continuation of the old League of Nations World Court, with headquarters in the same Palace of Justice at the Hague, capital of the Netherlands. Its responsibility is the settling of legal disputes between nations. These may involve boundaries, the rights of the citizens of one nation in another country, or the interpretation of an old treaty. Cases are brought to the Court voluntarily by the parties involved in a case, or by virtue of an advance declaration made by some nations to accept the Court's jurisdiction. Fifteen distinguished judges from as many countries preside over this World Court; they are appointed to it for a nine-year term, with the privilege of reappointment. Like the Security Council, the International Court of Justice is always in session.

The sixth and last main division of the United Nations is the Secretariat — the great body of workers who handle the day-by-day business of the organization. Among the more than four thousand of them, selected from all member nations, are doctors, lawyers, economists, scientists, diplomats, financiers, secretaries, librarians, researchers, and maintenance workers. Some are stationed in the buildings inherited from the old League of Nations in Geneva, but most of them work in the spectacular United Nations headquarters in New York.

At the head of this administrative force is the Secretary-General, elected by the General Assembly. There have been three Secretaries-General in the twenty-year history of the United Nations. Trygve Lie, a Norwegian, served the organization devotedly for its first seven years. Dag Hammarskjöld, from Sweden, followed Mr. Lie, dedicating himself to the pursuit of world peace from 1953 to his tragic death in 1961, while on a UN mission in Africa. U Thant, a Burmese diplomat, elected to fill out Mr. Hammarskjöld's term, was installed in his own right in 1962 for a five-year term.

The office of Secretary-General has developed into an executive and diplomatic position with worldwide influence.

The Secretary-General must keep posted on world affairs, administer the Secretariat, receive important delegations, and attend meetings of the General Assembly (to which he makes an annual report), the Security Council, and the Economic and Social Council. He also travels a great deal in order to explore troubled areas and discuss them with national leaders. Often he is able with skillful diplomacy to prevent threatening situations from reaching dangerous proportions.

The Secretary-General's office is at the top of the imposing United Nations Secretariat building overlooking New York's East River. With the other UN buildings which house the Assembly, the Councils, committees, and library, it was built on land donated by a wealthy, public-spirited American family and erected with the help of a loan from the United States Government. Always a busy place, the United Nations headquarters has become a real beehive since new member nations have more than doubled its size. Much of its work goes on outside the official meetings — in committees and as informal talks in corridors, on the lovely grounds, and in the attractive delegates' lounge and dining room. These contacts between informed national representatives play a big part in ironing out misunderstandings, cementing friendships, and achieving a peaceful world.

The fourteen specialized agencies sponsored by the Economic and Social Council carry on the United Nations work of banishing ignorance and poverty and increasing economic and social well-being "everywhere in the world." Membership in the agencies is purely voluntary. Some nations, like the United States, belong and contribute to all of them; other nations belong to only a few.

First of the specialized agencies is the FAO — Food and

Agriculture Organization — whose job is to relieve hunger and poverty everywhere, to raise living standards, to increase and distribute the world's supply of food so that no one anywhere will go hungry. Its experts examine soil and water resources, analyze food production, help improve crops, stamp out plant diseases, and increase milk production. Its many programs are practical ones, and its "freedom from hunger" campaign never ends.

WHO, the World Health Organization, is dedicated to the "attainment by all peoples of the highest possible level of health." Its workers are doing a big job independently and in cooperation with other agencies in fighting disease and spreading health information. Diseases like yaws, malaria, and leprosy have been wiped out in some areas with its help. Hospitals and health clinics are built and maintained by WHO in many countries.

UNICEF, which works closely with WHO, is not one of the specialized agencies. It was started right after the war as the United Nations International Children's Emergency Fund, but is now known simply as the UN Children's Fund. It concentrates on child health and care and the protection of mothers. Instead of getting funds from the UN, it is supported by Governments, private organizations, and individuals. Each country which benefits from its services contributes a share of the cost.

UNESCO, as its letters indicate, is the United Nations agency charged with raising standards in education, science, and culture. Universal elementary education is its first aim, since nearly half the children in the world do not go to any kind of school, and it has a well-planned teacher-training program. More knowledge, the UN knows, will increase efficiency as well as understanding and tolerance of other peoples.

The International Labor Organization (ILO) was connected with the old League of Nations and has worked with the United Nations since soon after its start. Its purpose is to improve working conditions and living standards throughout the world. It believes that "lasting peace can be established only if it is based on social justice."

Two specialized agencies are connected with communication — the Universal Postal Union (UPU) and the International Telecommunication Union (ITU). The World Meteorological Organization (WMO) is concerned with the weather; the Intergovernmental Maritime Consultative Organization (IMCO) with shipping and safety at sea; the International Civil Aviation Organization (ICAO) with navigation and safety in the air; and the International Atomic Energy Agency (IAEA) with "atoms for peace." The remaining specialized agencies work in the financial field — the International Bank for Reconstruction and Development (BANK), which resulted from the 1944 Bretton Woods Conference; the International Finance Corporation (IFC); the International Monetary Fund (IMF); and the International Development Association (IDA).

Each agency is separately organized, with its own charter, regulations, and headquarters. Day and night their consultants, technical experts, and clerical personnel are at work in many places all over the world, carrying out their special responsibility toward fulfilling the aim of the parent organization, the Economic and Social Council. This is "the creation of conditions of stability and well-being which are necessary for peaceful and friendly relations among nations."

Besides the agencies, the Economic and Social Council sponsors four regional and several other commissions, among them the Commission for Human Rights. This is the commission which prepared, under Eleanor Roosevelt's chairmanship, the Universal Declaration of Human Rights adopted by the General Assembly in 1948 and an important influence, especially in newer nations.

It is easy to become so interested in the progress of some special UN commission, agency, or activity that one loses sight of the accomplishments of the organization as a whole. The United Nations does not stand still while its agencies carry on impressive programs and projects "everywhere in the world." It has been able, to quote the late American Ambassador Adlai Stevenson, "to adapt to changing realities in world affairs; to begin to create workable international peace-keeping machinery; to begin to grapple with the complex problems of disarmament; to stimulate effective international cooperation."

Adapting to world changes has been no easy matter. Twenty years ago, when the United Nations was formed, the nuclear age had not begun, nor the exploration of outer space, nor the "cold war" between the world's two greatest powers — allies then and both charter members of the UN. In 1945, no one foresaw how the world would shrink with the speeding up of transportation and communication or how interdependent its nations would become. No one guessed at the emergence of Communist China or of the scores of smaller African and Asian nations. All these changes are felt in the United Nations. The friction between the Soviet Union and the United States has put strains on the smooth operation of the UN Charter. So has the doubling of members, and the consequent shifting of the balance of power to the smaller nations.

The year 1965 was marked by a grave dispute over whether the cost of UN peacekeeping operations should be voluntary or compulsory, by the Charter amendment increasing membership in the Security Council and the Economic and Social Council, and by Pope Paul VI's unprecedented appearance in New York to plead, "No more war, war never again!"

As world problems become more complicated, and with them the problems of the United Nations, the world's need for the organization grows. Secretary-General Dag Hammarskjöld recognized this need when he called the United Nations an "admittedly imperfect but indispensable instrument of nations in working for a peaceful evolution toward a more just and secure world order."

Already the UN has done much toward accomplishing its objectives of preventing war and promoting human rights, justice, and social progress. As peacemaker, it has kept a dozen or more situations from exploding into full-blown conflicts, and no one need be reminded of its role in Korea, Suez, the Congo, and Cyprus. Its patient pursuit of eventual disarmament has met with some success, and its International Court of Justice has contributed to the formulation and observance of international law. Through its agencies, the UN has raised economic, educational, and health standards throughout the world.

The United Nations has faced many crises and, to quote Mr. Stevenson again, has "emerged each time more mature and better able to face the next one." But Stevenson also reminded us that the UN is "like a spade; it is not self-operating . . . it is an opportunity only if we grasp it."

The future of the United Nations depends on its member nations — on the way they stand behind it, the use they make of its resources, and the confidence they place in its effectiveness as an agency for peacemaking and progress. Few things can be more important to every person on earth. For, in the words of the Philippine statesman Carlos Romulo, the United Nations is "mankind's best will for the building of a new kind of world — a free world, a secure world, a world at peace."

Let the word go forth from this time and place, to friend and foe alike, that the torch has been passed to a new generation of Americans—born in this century, tempered by war, disciplined by a hard and bitter peace, proud of our ancient heritage—and unwilling to witness or permit the slow undoing of those human rights to which this nation has always been committed, and to which we are committed today at home and around the world.

JOHN F. KENNEDY

Appendix I

IN THE FUTURE DAYS, which we seek to make secure, we look forward to a world founded upon four essential human freedoms.

The first is freedom of speech and expression—everywhere in the world.

The second is freedom of every person to worship God in his own way—everywhere in the world.

The third is freedom from want—which, translated into world terms, means economic understandings which will secure to every nation a healthy peacetime life for its inhabitants—everywhere in the world.

The fourth is freedom from fear—which, translated into world terms, means a worldwide reduction of armaments to such a point and in such a thorough fashion that no nation will be in a position to commit an act of physical aggression against any neighbor—anywhere in the world.

That is no vision of a distant millennium. It is a definite basis for a kind of world attainable in our own time and generation. That kind of world is the very antithesis of the so-called new order of tyranny which the dictators seek to create with the crash of a bomb.

To that new order we oppose the greater conception—the moral order. A good society is able to face schemes of world domination and foreign revolutions alike without fear.

Since the beginning of our American history we have been engaged in change—in a perpetual peaceful revolution—a revolution which goes on steadily, quietly adjusting itself to changing conditions—without the concentration camp or the quicklime in the ditch. The world order which we seek is the cooperation of free countries, working together in a friendly, civilized society.

This Nation has placed its destiny in the hands and heads and hearts of its millions of free men and women; and its faith in freedom under the guidance of God. Freedom means the supremacy of human rights everywhere. Our support goes to those who struggle to gain those rights or keep them. Our strength is in our unity of purpose.

To that high concept there can be no end save victory.

Appendix II

We the Peoples of the United Nations
Determined

to save succeeding generations from the scourge of war, which twice in our lifetime has brought untold sorrow to mankind, and

to reaffirm faith in fundamental human rights, in the dignity and worth of the human person, in the equal rights of men and women and of nations large and small, and

to establish conditions under which justice and respect for the obligations arising from treaties and other sources of international law can be maintained, and

to promote social progress and better standards of life in larger freedom,

And for These Ends

to practice tolerance and live together in peace with one another as good neighbors, and

to unite our strength to maintain international peace and security, and

to ensure, by the acceptance of principles and the institution of methods, that armed force shall not be used, save in the common interest, and

to employ international machinery for the promotion of the economic and social advancement of all peoples,

Have Resolved to Combine Our Efforts
to Accomplish These Aims.

Accordingly, our representative Governments, through representatives assembled in the city of San Francisco, who have exhibited their full powers found to be in good and due form, have agreed to the present Charter of the United Nations and do hereby establish an international organization to be known as the United Nations.

Signed on June 26, 1945,
by representatives of fifty-one nations,
and ratified by a majority
of nations, October 24, 1945.

A Select Bibliography

Cahn, Edmond, ed. *The Great Rights.* Macmillan, 1963.

Chafee, Zechariah, Jr. *The Blessings of Liberty.* Lippincott, 1956.

Commager, Henry Steele. *Crusaders for Freedom.* Doubleday, 1962.

Douglas, William O. *A Living Bill of Rights.* Doubleday, 1961.

Edman, Irwin. *Fountainheads of Freedom: The Growth of the Democratic Idea.* Reynal and Hitchcock, 1941.

Handlin, Oscar and Mary. *The Dimensions of Liberty.* Harvard University, 1961.

Konvitz, Milton R. *Fundamental Liberties of a Free People: Religion, Speech, Press, Assembly.* Cornell University, 1957.

Monaghan, Frank. *Heritage of Freedom: The History and Significance of the Basic Documents of American Liberty.* Princeton University, 1947.

Rutland, Robert A. *The Birth of the Bill of Rights, 1776–1791.* University of North Carolina, 1955.

I FREEDOM OF SPEECH

General

Chafee, Zechariah, Jr. *Free Speech in the United States.* Harvard University, 1941.

Douglas, William O. *The Right of the People.* Doubleday, 1958.

Hudon, Edward G. *Freedom of Speech and Press in America.* Public Affairs Press, 1963.

Jones, Howard M., ed. *Primer of Intellectual Freedom.* Harvard University, 1949.

John Peter Zenger

Buranelli, Vincent, ed. *The Trial of Peter Zenger.* New York University, 1957.

Galt, Tom. *Peter Zenger: Fighter for Freedom.* Crowell, 1951.

George Mason

Hill, Helen. *George Mason, Constitutionalist.* Harvard University, 1938.

Rowland, Kate Mason. *The Life of George Mason, 1725–1792.* 2 vols. Putnam, 1892.

Rutland, Robert A. *George Mason, Reluctant Statesman.* Colonial Williamsburg and Holt, 1961.

Elijah Parish Lovejoy

Dillon, Merton L. *Elijah P. Lovejoy, Abolitionist Editor.* University of Illinois, 1961.

Gill, John. *Tide Without Turning: Elijah P. Lovejoy and Freedom of the Press.* Starr King Press, 1958.

Sterling, Dorothy. *Forever Free: The Story of the Emancipation Proclamation.* Doubleday, 1963.

Oliver Wendell Holmes, Jr.

Bent, Silas. *Justice Oliver Wendell Holmes.* Vanguard, 1932.

Bowen, Catherine Drinker. *Yankee from Olympus: Justice Holmes and His Family.* Little, Brown, 1944.

Judson, Clara Ingram. *Mr. Justice Holmes.* Follett, 1956.

Marke, Julius J., ed. *The Holmes Reader.* Oceana, 1955.

The American Library Association

Blanshard, Paul. *The Right to Read: The Battle Against Censorship.* Beacon, 1955.

Douglas, William O. *Freedom of the Mind.* Doubleday, 1964.

Jennison, Peter. *Freedom to Read.* Public Affairs Press, 1963.

McKeon, Richard, Merton, Robert K., and Gellhorn, Walter. *The Freedom to Read.* Bowker, 1957.

II Freedom of Religion

General

Cuninggim, Merrimon. *Freedom's Holy Light.* Harper, 1955.

Greene, Evarts B. *Religion and the State.* New York University, 1941.

Pfeffer, Leo. *Church, State, and Freedom.* Beacon, 1953.

Sweet, William Warren. *The Story of Religions in America*. Harper, 1930.

Roger Williams

Eaton, Jeanette. *Lone Journey*. Harcourt, 1944.

Ernst, James. *Roger Williams: New England Firebrand*. Macmillan, 1932.

Winslow, Ola Elizabeth. *Master Roger Williams*. Macmillan, 1957.

The Lords Baltimore

Agle, Nan Hayden, and Bacon, Frances A. *The Lords Baltimore*. Holt, 1962.

Sioussat, Anne L. *Old Baltimore*. Macmillan, 1931.

Wilstach, Paul. *Tidewater Maryland*. Bobbs-Merrill, 1931.

William Penn

Dolson, Hildegarde. *William Penn, Quaker Hero*. Random House, 1961.

Gray, Elizabeth Janet. *Penn*. Viking, 1938.

Peare, Catherine Owens. *William Penn: A Biography*. Lippincott, 1957.

Thomas Jefferson and James Madison

Judson, Clara Ingram. *Thomas Jefferson: Champion of the People*. Follett, 1952.

Kimball, Marie. *Jefferson—The Road to Glory, 1743–1776*. Coward McCann, 1943.

Sheean, Vincent. *Thomas Jefferson, Father of Democracy*. Random House, 1953.

Wibberley, Leonard. *Young Man from the Piedmont*. Farrar, Straus, 1963.

Brant, Irving. *James Madison, Father of the Constitution*. Bobbs-Merrill, 1950.

Padover, Saul K., ed. *The Complete Madison: His Basic Writings*. Harper, 1953.

Wilkie, Katharine E., and Moseley, Elizabeth R. *Father of the Constitution: James Madison*. Messner, 1963.

National Conference of Christians and Jews

Pitt, James E. *Adventures in Brotherhood*. Farrar, Straus, 1955.

Straus, Roger Williams. *Religious Liberty and Democracy*. Willett, Clark, 1939.

III FREEDOM FROM WANT

General

Hoffman, Paul G. *World Without Want.* Harper, 1962.

Humphrey, Hubert H. *The Cause Is Mankind.* Praeger, 1964.

Paddock, William and Paul. *Hungry Nations.* Little, Brown, 1964.

Shonfield, Andrew. *The Attack on World Poverty.* Random House, 1960.

Jacob A. Riis

Riis, Jacob A. *The Making of an American.* Macmillan, 1901, 1961.

Ware, Louise. *Jacob A. Riis: Police Reporter, Reformer, Useful Citizen.* Appleton-Century, 1938.

Samuel Gompers

Gompers, Samuel. *Seventy Years of Life and Labor.* Dutton, 1925, 1957.

Selvin, David F. *Sam Gompers, Labor's Pioneer.* Abelard, 1964.

Julia Clifford Lathrop

Addams, Jane. *My Friend, Julia Lathrop.* Macmillan, 1935.

George Washington Carver

Holt, Rackham. *George Washington Carver.* Doubleday, 1943.

Graham, Shirley and Lipscomb, George D. *Dr. George Washington Carver, Scientist.* Messner, 1944.

Means, Florence Crannell. *Carver's George: A Biography of George Washington Carver.* Houghton, 1952.

White, Anne Terry. *George Washington Carver.* Random House, 1953.

The Peace Corps

Luce, Iris, ed. *Letters from the Peace Corps.* Luce, 1964.

Madow, Pauline, ed. *The Peace Corps.* H. W. Wilson, 1964.

IV FREEDOM FROM FEAR

General

Biddle, Francis. *The Fear of Freedom.* Doubleday, 1951.

Davenport, Russell W. *The Dignity of Man.* Harper, 1955.

Franklin Delano Roosevelt and Anna Eleanor Roosevelt

Burns, James MacGregor. *Roosevelt: The Lion and the Fox.* Harcourt, 1956.

Thomas, Henry. *Franklin Delano Roosevelt.* Putnam, 1962.

Weingast, David E. *Franklin D. Roosevelt, Man of Destiny.* Messner, 1952.

Douglas, Helen Gahagan. *The Eleanor Roosevelt We Remember.* Hill and Wang, 1963.

Roosevelt, Eleanor. *Autobiography.* Harper, 1961.

Steinberg, Alfred. *Mrs. R.: The Life of Eleanor Roosevelt.* Putnam, 1958.

Linus Carl Pauling

Pauling, Linus Carl. *No More War!* Dodd, Mead, 1958.

Martin Luther King, Jr.

Clayton, Edward T. *Martin Luther King: The Peaceful Warrior.* Prentice-Hall, 1964.

King, Martin Luther, Jr. *Stride Toward Freedom: The Montgomery Story.* Harper, 1958.

King, Martin Luther, Jr. *Why We Can't Wait.* Harper, 1964.

Reddick, L. D. *Crusader Without Violence: A Biography of Martin Luther King.* Harper, 1959.

The United Nations

Courlander, Harold. *Shaping Our Times: What the United Nations Is and Does.* Oceana, 1960.

Galt, Tom. *How the United Nations Works.* Crowell, 1965.

Munro, Sir Leslie. *United Nations: Hope for a Divided World.* Holt, 1960.

Savage, Katharine. *The Story of the United Nations.* Walck, 1962.

Index